Endorsements

Becoming Melchizedek Se

"Becoming Melchizedek" inspires us to consider our positional authority that comes with inherent responsibility. Charles reminds us that church life is neither a spectator sport nor the leadership function of a select few. This is a well-researched thought-provoking, prophetic, yet systematic approach to previously uncharted potential. This book truly reflects the Lord's instructive prayer for, "Thy Kingdom come," and "Thy will be done on earth as it is in heaven." This is a book you cannot simply read—you must take time to think your way through it. Thank you, Charles, for launching us into this unfolding journey of revelation towards the fullness of God's intended potential.
Pastor Gary W. Carter
Founding Apostle, Life Church and CEO, Gary Carter Inc.
Edmonton, Alberta, Canada

This book is right on time, as the Lord's timing is always perfect and it will bring to light and confirm to those that are going through the process of becoming a Melchizedek Priest that it is real and that they have been created by God for such a time as this. Charles has brought both heavenly experiences and earthly scholarly biblical research together to frame a new paradigm of what the Father is doing in the final move of God so that the end (and beginning) can come. I know what is written is sound because I have been on this journey myself. You will find no better navigator to guide you in this new movement than Charles and no better resource than this book.
Cyrus Kairos

I thoroughly enjoyed "Becoming Melchizedek" and found the material very profitable. I receive. I believe. I'm in! This book resonates with me and is a confirmation of what I have been experiencing. Thank you, Charles, for allowing me to review it.
Peter Kendrick

I find "Becoming Melchizedek" both fascinating and engaging and I appreciate the combination of research, personal encounter and implementation of information that is beginning to emerge on the topic. As we enter escalating global events, within the chapters are signposts to prepare for paradigm changes that do not compromise the truth of Jesus. I could take each chapter and reread to gather a new understanding. I do not believe all the questions that occur within these pages can be answered at once. Nevertheless, it is good food for thoughtful reflection, study and prayer.

Laura Harris

There have been things the Lord has shown me about my own ministry that I could not understand how this could happen until I read your book. Walking in the supernatural power of the Order of Melchizedek would allow these things to happen. Thank you, Charles for being willing to step out and take the risk and deliver this message the Lord has given you, and to also be used to introduce and to lead the way in training for this movement. Be encouraged and strengthened in the Lord. May we be found obedient and patient as we are lead to fulfill this awesome responsibility you are awakening us to. I pray for God's mighty hand of protection for you, your family, your ministry and all that you are given to do.

Greg Meyer

Called Forth Ministries

"Becoming Melchizedek" is timely, insightful and full of revelation. Charles Robinson is on the cutting-edge of what is God is establishing in the earth. I would strongly recommend this book to every believer who wants to understand the heavenly order of the priesthood and their role in it.

Michael A. Carney

1-7-16

Dear Estus,

Welcome to your life's purpose and to your new journey!

Love,
Charter

Business Men Fellowship (Non Denominational)
La Mesa Chapter #214
Denny's, Tuesday 7:30 a.m.
70th St. & Alvarado Road
It's Not Just Business
Gal. 5:13-15
Al Estus
Call: 760 707-3301

Completed
Read 2/10/16

The Canticles of The Order of Melchizedek

Becoming Melchizedek

Book I Foundations

Heaven's Priesthood
and
Your Journey

by DR. CHARLES ROBINSON

⇡SPIRIT-LED
 PUBLISHING

Copyright © 2015 by Melchizedek International, a DBA of WISE Ministries International

All rights reserved. No part of this publication may be reproduced, distributed, or transmitted in any form or by any means, including photocopying, recording, or other electronic or mechanical methods, without the prior written permission of the publisher, except in the case of brief quotations embodied in critical reviews and certain other noncommercial uses permitted by copyright law. For permission requests, write to the author, addressed "Attention: Permissions," Dr. Charles Robinson, info@coachmybusiness.com

Special discounts are available on quantity purchases by corporations, associations, and others. For details on orders by US trade bookstores and wholesalers, contact the author at the email address above.

Unless otherwise noted Scripture quotations are from THE HOLY BIBLE, NEW INTERNATIONAL VERSION®, NIV® Copyright © 1973, 1978, 1984, 2011 by Biblica, Inc.® Used by permission. All rights reserved worldwide.

Scripture quotations taken from the Amplified® Bible,
Copyright © 1954, 1958, 1962, 1964, 1965, 1987 by The Lockman Foundation Used by permission." (www.Lockman.org)

Scripture quotations are from The Holy Bible, English Standard Version® (ESV®), copyright © 2001 by Crossway, a publishing ministry of Good News Publishers. Used by permission. All rights reserved.

Scripture is taken from GOD'S WORD®, © 1995 God's Word to the Nations. Used by permission of Baker Publishing Group.

Scripture taken from the NEW AMERICAN STANDARD BIBLE®,
Copyright © 1960, 1962, 1963, 1968, 1971, 1972, 1973, 1975, 1977, 1995 by The Lockman Foundation. Used by permission.

The New Testament in Modern English
Scripture quotations marked "Phillips" are taken from The New Testament in Modern English, copyright � 1958, 1959, 1960 J.B. Phillips and 1947, 1952, 1955, 1957 The Macmillian Company, New York. Used by permission. All

rights reserved.

Verses from the Complete Jewish Bible by David H. Stern. Copyright © 1998. All rights reserved. Used by permission of Messianic Jewish Publishers, 6120 Day Long Lane, Clarksville, MD 21029. www.messianicjewish.net.

Scripture quotations marked "KJV" are taken from the Holy Bible, King James Version, Cambridge, 1769.

Scripture quotations from THE MESSAGE. Copyright © by Eugene H. Peterson 1993, 1994, 1995, 1996, 2000, 2001, 2002. Used by permission of Tyndale House Publishers, Inc.

Scripture quotations marked (TLB) are taken from The Living Bible copyright © 1971. Used by permission of Tyndale House Publishers, Inc., Carol Stream, Illinois 60188. All rights reserved.

Scripture quotations marked HCSB are taken from the Holman Christian Standard Bible®, Used by Permission HCSB ©1999,2000,2002,2003,2009 Holman Bible Publishers. Holman Christian Standard Bible®, Holman CSB®, and HCSB® are federally registered trademarks of Holman Bible Publishers.

Editor: Katherine Bell, freelancer

Cover designer: Marcelo Augusto Mascarenhas

Photo of Dr. Charles Robinson: Allison Metcalfe Photography

First Edition, 2015

ISBN: 978-1-943011-07-0

Publisher: Spirit-Led Publishing

Dedication

I dedicate this first work in The Order of Melchizedek Series to my wife, Liz, with thanks for her love, wisdom, and revelation; and to my son, Nathanael, who is a sign of the type of ministry God has called us to. Also, I was separated from Liz for almost two months while I wrote this book as I worked in China. Thank you, Liz, for your love and patience during this time. Your reward in heaven is equal to that of mine.

I further dedicate this work to my Lord and Savior, Yeshua, the only begotten Son of God, who is a priest forever after the Order of Melchizedek.

I finally dedicate this work to my dear friend, a mighty warrior, and my personal intercessor during the writing of this book, Cyrus Kairos. Cyrus, thank you for surrounding me with angels of protection and for your input on this book.

Table of Contents

Preface 1

Acknowledgements 10

Introduction 11

Five Assumptions 12
Who is This Guide For? 14
Prophetic Utterances 14
Proper Names Used 15
The 3rd Reformation 16
Note re: Pure Sources 17

Chapter 1: God's Heart: A Kingdom of Priests 18

God's Heart from the Beginning: A Kingdom of Priests 18
My Call: To Present You in Yeshua's Fullness to the Father ... 23
Three Dimensions of God 27
An Impenetrable Fortress 29
Walking as Yeshua Walked: 10,000 "Little Yeshua's" 29

Chapter 2: Who is Melchizedek? 31

What's in a Name? 31
An Order of Melchizedek? 31
There Were Two Distinct Groups of Levites 33
Treasurer of Heaven 35
Needed: Melchizedek Revelation 36
Melchizedek: the Hidden Wisdom of God 40
Unlocking the Mysteries 40
Melchizedek and Mysticism 44
The Dead Sea Scrolls Identify 45

iii

Chapter 3: Melchizedek Transformation 49
Abrahamic Encounter 49
   Establishment in God 49
   Blessing 50
   Change of Name Change of Nature 54
   Summary of Abram's Encounter 56
Melchizedek Transfiguration 57
   Jesus' Transfiguration 58
The Face of the Father 61

Chapter 4: The Melchizedek Priesthood 64
Yeshua's Own Order 64
Yeshua the Pattern Melchizedek Priest 65
Moses: a Melchizedek Before Yeshua 66
Priests, Prophets, Apostles, *and* Kings 67
   Melchizedek Evolution 68
Requirements for The Priesthood 69

1.   Righteousness 70
The Heavenly Garments 70
God is Activating Leaders 72

Chapter 5: The Purpose of Melchizedek 75
Dominion 75
   Release of the Greater Works 80
   Taking the Seven Mountains 81
Evangelism and the Great Harvest of Souls 87
   Salvation of the Jews 88
   Reaching Muslims for Yeshua 89

Chapter 6: School for Melchizedek's 91
Seven Years Under the Sevenfold Spirit 91

The Importance of the Baptism in Holy Spirit 94
   Scriptures Referring to Holy Spirit 95
WISE Melchizedek University Online... 97
Issachar Coaches and Intercessors 99
   The Issachar's 99
Mobilizing God's Generals 102

Chapter 7: Functions of The Melchizedek Order 107
Functioning in Fullness 107
King and Priest and Five-fold Anointing's Combined 110
   Melchizedek Priests as Leaders 110
   King and Priest... 112
Functions of The Priesthood.. 114
Introduction to Melchizedek Intercession 2.0................................... 118
   Intervention 120
The Eldership of the Earth 122
Introduction to Mystical Powers 124
   Working with Angels and Angel Armies 125

Chapter 8: The Church and Her Melchizedek Leaders 127
God is Going to Clean Up His Church 127
   Tithing... 128
   Preparation of the Bride 128
Introduction to the Church of Philadelphia..................................... 129
The Forerunner Anointing 130
The Nathanael Generation 132
Backlash 135
   Persecution 135
   Civil War in the Church? 136
Final Disobedience.. 137
   Lot Spirit.. 138

Chapter 9A: Priesthood Showdowns Coming 139
- Babylon 140
- Two Cities 141
- False Melchizedek's 142
- False Priesthoods 143
  - *The Catholic Church* *143*
  - *The Mormon Enterprise* *143*
  - *Islamic Clerics* *144*
  - *Other False Priests and Their Organizations* *144*
- Nephilim Societies/Aliens and UFO's 145
- 9B: The War Ahead 145
- The Order vs. the Forces of Hell 146
- The UN 146
- The New World Order and the Globalists 147
- Antichrist, Beast, and False Prophet 148
- Last Days' Anointing Against the Lawless Ones 149

Chapter 10: The Coming Kingdom Economy 152
- World Financial Meltdown 152
- The Transfer of Wealth 153
  - *Frozen Assets* *154*
- Transfer of Territory 155
- Gold Standard Stability 156

Chapter 11: Seeing Into Eternity 158
- Come Up Here: Revelation 4 Encounters 158
  - *The Brink of Eternity* *159*
- Melchizedek Transcends Time 159
  - *Timelessness in the Spirit or Being in the Moment with God* *161*
- Tasting the Powers of the Age to Come 164
  - *Portals* *164*

Breaking through Death 166
Amalgamation of Heaven and Earth 166
    Rapture 167
    An Appointment for Amalgamation Work 168
    Dual Action 169

Chapter 12: Melchizedek Manifested 171
The Godhead Within: An Impenetrable Fortress 171
Back to the Garden 171
The Restoration of the Three Mantles 172
Elijah/Elisha Acts of Power 172
Moses' Apostolic Fatherhood 173
The Joseph and Daniel Companies 173

Chapter 13: Resources: the Meat of Melchizedek 176
Melchizedek Comes By Revelation 176
The Qumran Vantage Point 176
    Melchizedek and the Dead Sea Scrolls 177
    Parallels with the Teachings of Jesus 183
The Need for Meat or Solid Food 183
Recommended Resources 186
    WISE Books/School for Melchizedek Forthcoming 186

APPENDIX A: Application to Melchizedek International 189

APPENDIX B: 7 MOUNTAINS PROPHECIES 2015 209

APPENDIX C: "Melchizedek" and "Salem" Etymologies 229

APPENDIX D: History of Jerusalem 237

Spirit-Led Publishing 245

Notes 246

More from WISE Ministries: 247

About the Author 248

Preface

"Those who are wise will shine like the brightness of the heavens, and those who lead many to righteousness, like the stars for ever and ever." (Daniel 12:3.)

Melchizedek International, www.Melchizedek.International, is a DBA of WISE Ministries International. WISE is a pioneer in the new "strategic intelligence" space, otherwise called "coaching and intercession for enterprises." WISE is helping to birth the "Spiritual Services" industry. Dr. Charles and Liz Robinson founded WISE Ministries International in 2005 to be a training, equipping, and service ministry to businesses, ministries, and enterprises in all seven mountains of culture. WISE provides intercession, kingdom consulting, and timely prophetic words in all seven of the spheres of culture. These spheres are sometimes referred to as the seven mountains of culture: business, government, arts & entertainment, media, education, family, and religion.

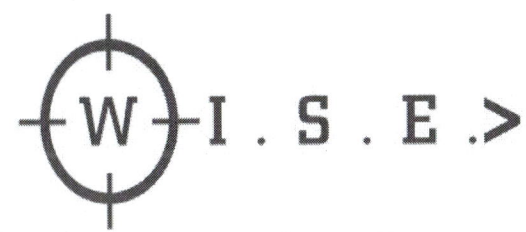

W.I.S.E.>

Workplace. Intercession. Support. Empowerment.™
Focused and Targeted Strategic Intelligence

WISE services provide a vibrant training, consulting, and healing ministry for developing and equipping the body of Yeshua to live in victory through experiencing the delivering power of Jesus, our Lord and Savior. WISE teaches people how to incorporate prayer into their enterprises, and trains and imparts into the next generation.

WISE is active in:

Government—by supporting local and national candidates, by impacting the governmental mountain through DC-based intercessory teams, and through its Gates2DC.com ministry;

Arts & Entertainment—through the Gates2Hollywood.com ministry and association with several major Christian film studios and their releases;

Family—through its marriage counseling ministry;

Education—through its ministry at foundational universities such as Harvard University and its own Seven Mountains University and Melchizedek International;

Business—through the entrance, via intercession and/or coaching, into over one hundred companies in numerous industries.

Religion—through support of church and parachurch ministries; and

Media—via Internet and satellite on The Way Network and The Cross Network, networks that cover the globe with access to over 120 million people.

WISE employs intercessors and coaches all over the world in a decentralized model, utilizing the latest in Internet technologies for communication. **WISE** teaches people how to incorporate prayer into their enterprises.

WISE maintains offices in Hollywood, California; Washington, D.C.; and Shenzhen, China. We can also travel to enterprises for on-site initial consultations, assessments, and evaluations.

How WISE Got Started

In 2005, I, Charles, was invited to attend the International Christian Chamber of Commerce yearly meeting in Washington, D.C. Leaders from all walks of life, local and international, were present. I, along with others, ministered to these leaders for hours by the Spirit. The anointing and power of God were very strong. It was there that God birthed WISE. God gave Liz the name, "WISE," which stands for "Workplace Intercession, Support, and Empowerment." WISE empowers marketplace leaders and their employees by helping them fulfill their callings in their businesses and other enterprises.

We composed "Empowering You for Success" as our slogan, and chose Daniel 12:3 as our company Scripture: *"Those who are wise will shine like the brightness of the heavens, and those who lead many to righteousness, like the stars for ever and ever."*

At that same ICCC meeting, I met a special couple from Tuscaloosa, Alabama: Fred and Dorinda Trick. Before this meeting, Liz had attended training on intercession with Elizabeth Alves of Increase International, and one of her modules was on how to pray for businesses. Surprisingly, this couple said to me that they were thinking about contacting that ministry to find an intercessor to pray for their business. I promptly responded that I knew just the person, and it was Liz, my wife!

Shortly after Liz and I had launched a new church in Austin, Texas, the Lord said that He was going to give me the corporate anointing. I asked the Lord what that meant as I thought this was perhaps related to becoming a day trader in stocks or some other related pursuit. However, the Lord said that He was going to expand WISE and that the corporate anointing was for bringing His presence and His power into companies—both large and small.

While we pastored our church, God let us know that He wanted us to take His presence and power outside the four walls of the church and into the marketplace. He was going to use our business, entrepreneurial, management, and leadership skills to let heaven invade the seven mountains of culture. (Hence the title of our course.)

Our Background

At the time of this writing, we (Charles and Liz) have brought the Word of the Lord to thousands of people. As we are experienced church and corporate pastors, intercessors, chaplains, teachers, and business owners, we with our team of intercessors and business consultants are equipped to support and empower you and your ministry for success. In 2005, we founded a dynamic local church in Austin, TX, where we served together as senior pastors for five years.

We are now corporate pastors to many organizations, both nationally and internationally, empowering them to impact all seven mountains where they have influence. We are committed to and passionate about training and imparting the wisdom, understanding, and experience the Lord has given us. Our mission is to develop strong, mature ambassadors and warriors for Yeshua, and to bring the saving knowledge of Jesus to our nation and the nations of this world.

Together we have over four decades of collective business and managerial experience. We are ordained ministers with the Christian International Ministries Network. I (Charles) minister regularly through the Gates2Hollywood and Gates2DC Ministries, and I have experience as a talk radio and Christian television host in central Texas. I am the director of the International Apostolic Marketplace Intercessors Network (IAMIN), which provides a training ground, network, referrals, and certification for marketplace intercessors. The IAMIN is advised by an external board of directors all with a broad base of marketplace ministry experience.

We both have Bible theology training, and I (Charles) possess a doctorate in theology (2013), Divinity (2014), and a

Ph.D. in Theology (2015). Also, I am the chancellor of the online Seven Mountains University (7MU.school) and the CEO of Melchizedek International (www.Melchizedek.international). In addition, I hold an associate in business data processing and am the CEO of nonprofit and for-profit companies. I am a professional level intercessor, certified professional coach, and a certified crisis chaplain. Liz has a BS in business administration with a concentration in marketing.

I am the founder of the Economically Tested Financiers (ETF) Forum and the convener of the annual Tipping Point Gathering 7-UP Unconference. I'm also an ambassador for the International Coalition of Apostolic Leaders—ICAL USA, The United States Coalition of Apostolic Leaders under Apostles John Kelly and Joseph Mattera, and a member of the Global Spheres Network led by Apostles Chuck Pierce and Peter Wagner.

Certification Courses

WISE currently offers five certification courses in a series called "Let Heaven Invade the Seven Mountains of Culture."

Other Existing and Planned Volumes

Volume 1: WISE 7M Intercessor Certification Guide certifies Professional Level Intercessors.

Volume 2: WISE 7M Leadership Certification Guide informs CEO's and business and organizational leaders on how to implement spiritual services within their organizations. Specifically, the guide instructs leaders how to identify, engage, manage, and release intercessors, corporate pastors, spiritual coaches, and chief revelatory officers into their organizations for their corporate and personal well-being.*

Volume 3: WISE 7M Coaching Certification Guide with spiritual coach, life coach, executive coach, and executive leadership coaching options.†

Volume 4: WISE 7M Chaplain Certification Guide is for those corporate pastors who are called to minister to the needs of employees of organizations large and small.

Volume 5: WISE 7M General's Certification Guide is for the top marketplace leaders in all seven mountains who need the best in "spiritual survival" training—for dealing with all kinds of spiritual dilemmas. Leaders learn how to deal with (take authority over and get to the root of) many situations that can arise in their global enterprises.‡

Course Schedule and Format Options

Certification courses start monthly. Check markteplaceintercessors.com, marketplaceceos.com, marketplacecoaches.com and/or marketplacegenerals.com for prices and offering dates.

All five of the courses listed above are available in two formats: Group and Fast Track with two-and-a-half days of live on-site training coupled with **Independent Study.** All modules are divided over twelve weeks. Both formats offer the student impartation, wisdom, and experience from personal contact with WISE instructors.

* See marketplaceCEOS.com for more information.
† See marketplacecoaches.com for more information.
‡ See marketplacegenerals.com for more information.

Our main prayer websites: prayformybusiness.com prayformyministry.com	Our intercessor certification: IAMCERT.com marketplaceintercessors.com
Our 7M sites: tippingpointgathering.com 7MCouncil.com charlesrobinson.me 7MU.school Seven Mountains University 7MInstitute.com JosephRegistry.com	Our coaching sites: coach4mylife. marketplacecoaches.com coachmybusiness.com**

WISE provides monthly newsletters in "The Joseph Blog," available at:

CoachMyBusiness.com/marketplace-ministry

The 7M book series is available at the site:

LetHeavenInvade7M.com

Site to purchase Melchizedek books and everything Melchizedek:

Melchizedek.International

§ See marketplaceintercessors.com, and iamcert.com for more information.

Acknowledgements

Special thanks to my editor. Katherine Bell, freelancer, did the editing of *Becoming Melchizedek Book I, Foundations.* Katherine holds a B.A. in English from Davidson College as well as a Doctor of Ministry from Christian Life School of Theology Global. She has also completed course work in writing and editing from UNC School of Journalism and UC Berkeley Extension. As a writer/ghostwriter/editor/researcher, Katherine brings a great depth in the Word and Christian thought plus a rich life in Yeshua to her work. Her heart is to see *"the earth . . . full of the knowledge of the Lord, as the waters cover the sea."* (Isaiah 11:9 TLB.) She lives and prays on campus at morningstarministries.org in Fort Mill, SC. Contact her at katherinefbell@me.com.

Special gratitude to all of our clients and friends. The partnerships and friendships with you have impacted Liz and me in ways that only God knows. This work is a testimony to the lessons learned as we have worked together.

We also thank Allison Metcalfe of Allison Metcalfe Photography and design for her photo of Dr. Charles Robinson in the About the Author section.

Introduction

First this is a revelatory work. Its words come from visions, encounters, and the like. At the same time, my full intent is to stay true to the inerrant Word of God. This work is Biblically sound. It is unique within the canon of Melchizedek knowledge in that it addresses current events plus draws a prophetic picture of the future as it substantiates the need for a priesthood from heaven to answer head-on the global challenges of our day.

What you have is *Book I of The Canticles of The Order of Melchizedek, Becoming Melchizedek, Foundations.* A canticle is a hymn or chant typically using words from the Bible. A canticle has definite structure and order. In the liturgy of churches such as the Eastern Orthodox and others, canticles established the mood of the day, the order or flow of things. There is a tone in the calling of God re: how someone is introduced to The Order of Melchizedek and how that someone accepts and grows in His or her knowledge of The Order. Let this Book I be a canticle of the new tone and song of your life—the song the Lord is birthing within you. A canticle now in heaven and coming to earth.

Through this book you are now able to answer the Revelation 4:1 call of God to, *"Come up here and I will show you things to come,"* in order to become the Father's priest on the earth—someone to represent Him and minister to Him. Father has always wanted this from time immemorial. His desire even dates back to when He placed Adam and Eve in the Garden of Eden.

As I write this introduction, it's the beginning of Hebrew year 5776, and today, September 27th, 2015, is actually the last blood moon of the tetrad. So what could be more prophetic than the birthing of this Order of Melchizedek how-to manual and even a "what's next" manual at this time? I note Daniel 12:3, *"Those who are wise will shine like the brightness of the heavens, and those who lead many to righteousness, like the stars for ever and ever."*

What is an Order of God? An Order represents a reality as it exists in heaven. It is a structure of God or an existing function, such as the temple in heaven and its ministering priests. We know from Hebrews that the heavenly pattern is superior to its earthly manifestation. The heavenly Melchizidekian priesthood, much superior to the Levitical, has always existed. In Psalm 110 and in Hebrews 7, God said of Yeshua, *"You are a High Priest appointed forever according to The Order of Melchizedek."* It is now time for heaven's priestly administration to come to earth with Yeshua as its head. The coming of The Order is next in the spiritual-evolutionary journey. Now is its time.

Five Assumptions

As I write this book, I make the following five assumptions about you.

Assumption 1: You may or may not be a Christian right now. And you do not need to be a Christian believer to benefit from this book. But, you are spiritually minded and open to the realm of possibilities. It's good to be open to new truths, too. I promise I will not try to convert you to Christianity, but if you read this material, I warn you that you may want to become a Christian in order to walk into the fullness of The Order of Melchizedek.

Assumption 2: You desire to serve heaven, people, and God Himself on earth as a king and priest after The Order of Melchizedek. You may not know all that this entails, but you are willing and open to what God has for you.

Assumption 3: You are willing to extend grace and be persistent. I realize that the methods I describe in this book are unorthodox or not what some would consider mainstream. To me, that is exactly why they work. We need new solutions to problems both old and new. The new solutions and methods can be found in the ancient paths. I have made every attempt to make this treatise approachable and Biblical.

Assumption 4: You approach this topic with an open mind and a teachable spirit. You might not be of a Charismatic Christian background. But this book is still for you! We can work around our differences through God's grace and a desire for unity. Please do not let any disagreement stop you from reading this material.

Assumption 5: Reading this book will not make you a Melchizedek Priest. God, Himself, must call you on this journey. However, this book will help you discover *if* you have been called on this journey and then equip you for God's service. It will be an invaluable resource for you. Thereafter will be a lot of custom personal training and specialized curricula that God will have for you as well, based upon your specialty in The Melchizedek Priesthood. The existence of these specializations is known by revelation. Be prepared, God is going to mess you up with this book. In a good way.

Who is This Guide For?

This guide was written to impart spiritual truth to individuals who feel called to the ministry of The Order of Melchizedek. You will be trained in a step-by-step approach that will feed you systematically. Lessons come from both from my life, and lessons come directly from God.

Prophetic Utterances

There are at least nine prophetic utterances in this book. Actually, you may think of the entire book as a prophetic word. Along with these direct words from God, God had to inspire much of the book as much of the material is virgin—straight from the throne and never published before. (And I claim this with holy fear.) When I use someone else's material, I cite the source. God has truly directed the words used and the progression of this book. Prophetic words are given just as I received them from God. They all begin with **"Word of the Lord."**

Proper Names Used

I use the names Yeshua, Jesus, the Lamb, and Christ interchangeably. But the Son of God's name is truly Yeshua or Yahshua if you prefer. For the name of God the Father, I use God, g-d, YHWH, El Elyon (God Most High), or "the Father." I believe that the Tetragrammaton YHWH is His name and that is what I use in this book. Some prefer YHVH. Holy Spirit is just that, Holy Spirit. Also the Holy Spirit is the seven Spirits of God, the Spirits that comprise Holy Spirit. The name or title of Melchizedek (as used in this work) has been spelled Melchisedec, Melchisedek, Melchisedech, etc. By the way, the correct Hebrew pronunciation I am told sounds like "Mel-ka-ZA-dec" with the stress on the "ZA".

Seven Mountains refers to seven spheres in the earth. They are business/economy/finance, religion including all religions not just Christianity, media, arts and entertainment/sports, government/healthcare, family/marriage, and education. Family/marriage needs to be at the very base since without the fundamental family unit intact, society breaks down. Ultimately, God's mountain of Zion will fill and overshadow all these other mountains with the New Jerusalem, the Holy City (which is eternally tied to Melchizedek), at the center and even providing its own light.

For brevity, many times I use "The Priesthood" and "The Order" as abbreviations instead of spelling out "The Order of

Melchizedek." The name satan is purposely not capitalized, the least of which he has to worry about.

The 3rd Reformation

For centuries God in His infinite love and mercy has restored the church. The reformer Martin Luther delivered the truth that faith and not works saves man. From Luther, *"The just shall live by faith,"* was restored. God restored the gifts of the Spirit through the Azusa Street outpourings in the 1900's. In the 1950's, healing gifts resurfaced. Through the last decades of the twentieth century, apostles and prophets were reestablished in the Body. All reformational movements build upon revelatory, present truth. 2 Peter 1:12 KJV says, *"Wherefore I will not be negligent to put you always in remembrance of these things, though ye know them, and be established in the present truth."* Dr. Bill Hamon has illuminated this concept of the progressive uncovering of truth in his books, *The Eternal Church* and *Prophetic Scripture Yet to be Fulfilled: During the 3rd and Final Reformation*. Today, according to Hamon, we are living in "the day of the saints"—a time when the saints will take the kingdoms of this world and make them the kingdom of our Lord as prophesied in Revelation 11:15. The average saint will move in more power than the greatest ministers of today. And the Melchizedek Order is needed to lead! (See also Hamon's book, *The Day of the Saints: Equipping Believers for Their Revolutionary Role in Ministry.*)

Bishop Hamon is my bishop as Liz and I are ordained through the Christian International Apostolic Network.

Now is the time, and this is the book and the ministry to establish you in the *present truth* for your *full enablement* and *full embodiment* of God's ancient priesthood.

Note re: Pure Sources
Please note: I did not review or research any portion of the Book of Mormon as a source for this series. The name Melchizedek is mentioned in the Second Book of Enoch but since it is apocryphal I do not cite it nor does the content add or subtract from this work other than it saying that Melchizedek will be the head of the priests in a future generation which is interesting. Nor were New Age or any other extra-Biblical sources used other than the Dead Sea Scrolls. I believe that all prophetic inspiration was given me by Holy Spirit and should be tested according to the Biblical example.

Chapter 1: God's Heart: A Kingdom of Priests

God's Heart from the Beginning: A Kingdom of Priests

On Mount Sinai God issued an invitation: *"And ye shall be unto me a kingdom of priests, and an holy nation. These are the words which thou shalt speak unto the children of Israel."* (Exodus 19:6 KJV.) These were the very words of God to Israel even before they received the Ten Commandments. As a priest serves as an intermediary between God and men, so this "kingdom of priests" had been called by God to bring God's Word to mankind. With such a high calling as a holy nation, the people should have been holy, consecrated to God in life and witness. Let us also read the context of the call from Exodus 19:1-25.

> *On the first day of the third month after the Israelites left Egypt—on that very day—they came to the Desert of Sinai. After they set out from Rephidim, they entered the Desert of Sinai, and Israel camped there in the desert in front of the mountain. Then Moses went up to God, and the LORD called to him from the mountain and said, "This is what you are to say to the descendants of Jacob and what you are to tell the people of Israel: You yourselves have seen what I did to Egypt, and how I carried you on eagles' wings and brought you to Myself. Now if you obey me fully and keep my covenant, then out of all nations you will be my treasured possession. Although the whole earth is Mine, you will be for me a kingdom of priests and a holy nation. These are the words you are to speak to the*

Israelites." So Moses went back and summoned the elders of the people and set before them all the words the LORD had commanded him to speak. The people all responded together, "We will do everything the LORD has said." So Moses brought their answer back to the LORD. The LORD said to Moses, "I am going to come to you in a dense cloud, so that the people will hear me speaking with you and will always put their trust in you." Then Moses told the LORD what the people had said. And the LORD said to Moses, "Go to the people and consecrate them today and tomorrow. Have them wash their clothes and be ready by the third day, because on that day the LORD will come down on Mount Sinai in the sight of all the people. Put limits for the people around the mountain and tell them, 'Be careful that you do not approach the mountain or touch the foot of it. Whoever touches the mountain is to be put to death. They are to be stoned or shot with arrows; not a hand is to be laid on them. No person or animal shall be permitted to live. Only when the ram's horn sounds a long blast may they approach the mountain.'"

After Moses had gone down the mountain to the people, he consecrated them, and they washed their clothes. Then he said to the people, "Prepare yourselves for the third day. Abstain from sexual relations." On the morning of the third day there was thunder and lightning, with a thick cloud over the mountain, and a very loud trumpet blast. Everyone in the camp trembled. Then Moses led the people out of the camp to meet with God, and they stood at the foot of the mountain. Mount Sinai was covered with smoke, because the LORD descended on it in fire. *The smoke billowed up from it like smoke from a furnace, and the whole mountain trembled violently. As the sound of the trumpet grew louder and louder, Moses spoke and the voice of God answered him with thunder. The LORD descended to the top of Mount Sinai and called Moses to the top of the mountain. So Moses went up and the LORD said to him, "Go down and warn the people so they do not force their way through to see the LORD and many of them perish. Even the priests, who approach the LORD, must consecrate themselves, or the LORD will break out against them." Moses said to the LORD, "The people cannot come up Mount Sinai, because you yourself warned us, 'Put limits around the mountain and set it apart as holy.'" The LORD replied, "Go down and bring Aaron up with you. But the priests and the people must not force their way through to come up to the LORD, or He will break out against them." So Moses went down to the people and told them.*

Then on Sinai God gave the Ten Commandments. From Exodus 20:1-3.
"And God spoke all these words:
'I am the Lord your God, who brought you out of Egypt, out of the land of slavery.'

God's Heart: A Kingdom of Priests

'You shall have no other gods before me.'

And the rest. What was it like to encounter the living God? From verses 20 and 24, not all could come near. They were afraid of the voice of God. Exodus 20:18-21 records:

> *When the people saw the thunder and lightning and heard the trumpet and saw the mountain in smoke, they trembled with fear. They stayed at a distance and said to Moses, "Speak to us yourself and we will listen. But do not have God speak to us or we will die." Moses said to the people, "Do not be afraid. God has come to test you, so that the fear of God will be with you to keep you from sinning." The people remained at a distance, while Moses approached the thick darkness where God was.*

Since the Garden of Eden, it has always been in the heart of God to have a people who would minister to Him—a people who would be close. God's heart is no separation between Him, the Father, and us, His children. Moreover, it has always been the Father's objective to make His people into a kingdom of priests.

In Exodus, God invited His people to come near to speak with Him. God did not want to have to say as He did with the prophets, *"Listen to what I say: when there is a prophet among you, I, Adonai, make myself known to him in a vision, I speak with him in a dream. But it isn't that way with my servant Moshe. He is the only one who is faithful in my entire household. With him I speak face to face and clearly, not in riddles; he sees the image of Adonai."* (Numbers 12:6-8 CJB.) With Moses, it was face to face.

What is it about speaking with God face to face? This is the essence of The Order of Melchizedek—direct encounter with God. God showed His absolute awesomeness on the mount; there were thunders and lightning's just like in the throne room in heaven. (See Revelation 4:5.) The people saw this display of awesomeness and were greatly afraid. They had a fear of the supernatural, and, therefore, they said, "You, Moses, go and speak for us." That was their mistake. God wants *all* of His people to be close and to become His priests. It is only because of this halting that there arose a need for the Levitical and Aaronic Priesthoods. God never wanted to be separated from His people. They refused to come close, so God withdrew Himself to abide in the Holiest of Holies over the Ark of the Covenant within the veil of the Tabernacle where only the High Priest entered.

God instituted the Levitical Priesthood because the people refused to fellowship with Him themselves. So they needed to be kept in line. What they could have learned from God themselves, they now were spoon-fed by Moses and the Levitical Priesthood. God would have written His law on their hearts even in Old Testament times. (See Romans 2:15.) Yet, God was exhibiting one of His most necessary and prevalent attributes—patience. (Source: Perry, Dr. David. 2013. *Back to the Melchizedek Future.* Raleigh: Lulu.)

My Call: To Present You in Yeshua's Fullness to the Father

My call is to bring you into the fullness of encounter with Abba as consecrated Melchizedek Priests. To present a priesthood to the Father. I in no way feel adequate to do this. The Lord knows my heart. I, myself, am on this Melchizedek journey. But I do know that Hebrews 2:10 KJV says, *"For it became Him, for whom are all things, and by whom are all things, in bringing many sons unto glory, to make the captain of their salvation perfect through sufferings."* Yeshua had to suffer to birth sons. And I have had to suffer many things to get to the point of who I am today. I am still not perfect—just ask Liz, my wife.

Jesus is the captain of our salvation, and our captain has commissioned me to write this book, which, like the work of Jesus, is going to bring many sons unto glory. Jesus is going to use this book to bring you unto glory. This revelation is going to free you and empower you to become what you have waited all of your life to become. This book is going to remove limits and boundaries off of you. Just believe! Just receive! I have read many books that changed my life and helped me go to the next level. So, it is with this book and you. I must bring you into *"that measure of development which is meant by the 'fullness of Yeshua'"* as Yeshua and the seven Spirits are bringing me into it. (Ephesians 4:13 PHILLIPS.) I have gone ahead. Some of you may actually be ahead of me. That's OK; send me your thoughts and your experiences as I want to know about them. This work will be a living book. I will make revisions as my experience and your experience in The Order grows. I was told prophetically by an intercessor to hold nothing back. So I won't even though this material is nuclear and explosive and will turn some people on their heads.

What happened in the Book of Acts where it was said of Jesus' disciples that they turned the world upside down is coming again. (Acts 17.) The Order is going to turn the world right side up again. We live in an age where many *"call evil good, and good evil; they put darkness for light, and light for darkness."* (Isaiah 5:20.) *"As it was in the days of Noah...."* (Matthew 24:37.) We are up against a spirit of twisting and perversion—the leviathan spirit of Isaiah 27:1 that twists everything. This serpent spirit uses fear and dread to intimidate and silence believers. The Order will fight. Also Melchizedek has come to fulfill Luke 1:17—the turning of *"the hearts of the fathers to the children, and the disobedient to the wisdom of the just; to make ready a people prepared for the Lord."* The Melchizedek Company will break curses over the earth and its societies.

You and I in The Order are moving from glory to glory (2 Corinthians 3:18) and from faith to faith in God (Romans 1:17.) There will be meetings of The Order the Lord is showing me now. A training institute for The Order and for God's Generals. Marketplace training for world market penetration by kingdom enterprises. A place of refuge for The Order. We will be known as The Priesthood.

We will not be like the false priests and shepherds. Ezekiel stated God's words against them. From Ezekiel 34:2-13:

> *Son of man, prophesy against the shepherds of Israel; prophesy and say to them "This is what the Sovereign LORD says: Woe to you shepherds of Israel who only take care of yourselves! Should not shepherds take care of the flock? You eat the fat and clothe yourselves with the wool, you slaughter the fat sheep without feeding the flock. Those who are sickly you have not strengthened, the diseased you have not healed, the broken you have not bound up, the scattered you have not brought back, nor have you sought for the lost; but with force and with severity you have dominated them. They were scattered for lack of a shepherd, and they became food for every beast of the field and were scattered. My flock wandered through all the mountains and on every high hill; My flock was scattered over all the surface of the earth, and there was no one to search or seek for them." Therefore, you shepherds, hear the word of the LORD: "As I live," declares the Lord GOD, "surely because my flock has become a prey, my flock has even become food for all the beasts of the field for lack of a shepherd, and my shepherds did not search for my flock, but rather the shepherds fed themselves and did not feed my flock;" therefore, you shepherds, hear the word of the LORD. Thus says the Lord GOD, "Behold, I am against the shepherds, and I will demand my sheep from them and make them cease from feeding sheep. So the shepherds will not feed themselves anymore, but I will deliver my flock from their mouth, so that they will not be food*

> *for them." For thus says the Lord GOD, "Behold, I Myself will search for my sheep and seek them out. As a shepherd cares for his herd in the day when he is among his scattered sheep, so I will care for my sheep and will deliver them from all the places to which they were scattered on a cloudy and gloomy day. I will bring them out from the peoples and gather them from the countries and bring them to their own land; and I will feed them on the mountains of Israel, by the streams, and in all the inhabited places of the land."*

This passage speaks of the Hebrews returning to Israel and also of *"my flock."* Such is the heart of the Lord for His sheep, and such is the heart of a true Melchizedek Priest/Shepherd. It's said of Elijah that he will restore all things. (Matthew 17:11.) The heart of Elijah, of Elisha, of Joseph, of Daniel and the heart of Moses, is in the heart of the true Shepherd/Priests whom God is raising up. I, too, have a shepherd's heart. I want to see you restored. I want to see God's government increase and the foundations of His throne of righteousness and justice restored. I want to see truth and fairness restored to the seven mountains of culture. Melchizedek can do this because Melchizedek is God's arm of government. Melchizedek is God's scepter—His rod of authority. Speaking of the Lord who came out of the tribe of Judah, Genesis 49:10 KJV, declares, *"The sceptre shall not depart from Judah, nor a lawgiver from between his feet, until Shiloh come; and unto Him shall the gathering of the people be."*

God is going to gather His people back unto Himself. The Order will help accomplish this. And God will use true shepherds—those he can trust with His people and His resources.

Three Dimensions of God

There are three dimensions of God that we can see. By understanding and entering into the full development that is ours in Yeshua, by seeking greater revelation and encounter, we can again walk the earth in union and communion with the Godhead.

The first dimension of God came to us through the revelation of Jesus as a picture of God in the flesh over 2000 years ago. Jesus said, "*If you have seen me you have seen the Father.*" (John 14:9.) So, in Jesus dwelt all of the fullness that is in the Father, Son and Holy Spirit—the fullness of the Godhead. (Colossians 2:9.) He is to us what Father once was to Israel through His residence in the tabernacle—God with us or within us. Each of us His temple.

The second dimension was experienced in modern times through the outpouring of the Holy Spirit in the early 1900's and later revivals. As the second dimension—the filling or baptism of the Holy Spirit—was a geometric expansion of Jesus' presence as He came to indwell believers on the Day of Pentecost empowering them to touch the whole world so will this final release of Jesus' own power and authority to The Order of

Priests be also a geometric expansion. Note: Only those specifically prepared in the crucible of humility and hiddenness can and will enter in. It's not for every believer. Thus, I am not referring to The Priesthood of all believers, the truth of the access to God and the ministry call on everyone generally. This Priesthood is Jesus' own Order, and this Order will in turn call the multitudes to come up higher in God.

Put another way, if you compare the ministry of Jesus before He ascended and sent the Holy Spirit—one man in one place at a time—to Jesus' ministry after the Spirit's outpouring with the Holy Spirit now indwelling a corporate Body of Yeshua, you begin to see the impact that is coming under this new priesthood designated to walk in full power. As Nita Johnson puts it, "The Third Dimension is the revealing of The Priesthood of Melchizedek or Jesus operating in the fullness of power and authority through the Priests of His Order." (Source: (LaFond) Johnson, Nita. 2008. *Melchizedek the New Millennium Priesthood*. Fresno: World for Jesus Ministries.)

The Father will fully glorify His Son through this priesthood. Concurrently, we will also see the fullness of manifestation of the Father dwelling on the inside of man as well as He did with Adam. So this priesthood will also be part of a move of God the Father coming to tabernacle with men once again. He's coming down to abide with us forever.

An Impenetrable Fortress
God will become a fortress on the inside of His people. He will be an impenetrable fortress and a literal *foundation within* of the kingdom in full. Glorious manifestations are coming principally through His apostles and prophets, and Davidic *"mighty men of valor"* (1 Chronicles 5:24.) According to Nita Johnson, the Priests of The Order of Melchizedek will follow these *"mighty men of valor."*

Walking as Yeshua Walked: 10,000 "Little Yeshua's"
The term Christian means "Little Christ" Even put another way, imagine with the release of the Melchizedek anointing 10,000 Jesus's walking the earth at the same time in our age. We cannot even fathom it yet, but this happening is at the door. Whether people accept Yeshua as the only Savior or not, the whole world will experience the witness that Jesus Christ is Lord.

Chapter 2: Who is Melchizedek?

What's in a Name?

The name Melchizedek comes from two Hebrew words. First "Melchi" ("Melek" in Hebrew) means "king." "Melek" also conveys the sense of a title in that it can mean "chief chancellor." And "Zedek" ("Sadeq" in Hebrew) means "righteousness." Melchizedek is the King of Righteousness. He was also a priest—the Priest of the Most High God. He was a progenitor, a man next in line after Noah as a righteous man who preserved God's ways of heaven on the earth for future generations. Melchizedek was the king of Salem. He was involved in the earliest founding of the city that would be renamed Jerusalem, the City of our God and the City of David. King David would rule from this city, and soon our King of Glory, Yeshua, will also rule from David's throne city—Jerusalem. It's up to His Order to get Him to this throne. You may say, "But God is going to bring Him the throne." Yes, but through us, His Priesthood. We are going to pave the way for Him.

Please see the APPENDIX C for the etymology of the name Melchizedek and the word Salem. It is good reading and a good word study.

An Order of Melchizedek?

Genesis says that Abraham met this King-Priest Melchizedek in the Valley of the Kings and tithed unto him. Scripture goes on to say that Melchizedek was *"made like unto the Son of God."*

(Hebrews 7:3.) What does this mean? Perhaps it means made with a spiritual body like the pre-incarnate Jesus in heaven. Melchizedek cannot have been a theophany or a physical appearance of Yeshua before His birth and time on earth. Jesus was begotten or birthed by God the Father; He was never created as 7:3 says of Melchizedek. So the one whom Abraham met cannot have been Yeshua. Who else could it have been? Melchizedek was Shem, son of Noah, who founded the city Salem later named Jerusalem or City of Peace. Shem and Abraham were contemporaries. Shem was a Melchizedek representative of God before Yeshua. But, you may say "Shem had a father and mother?" Yes, Noah and Mrs. Noah (her name is not known for sure). That is true, however, having no beginning and no ending is referring to the *eternal* nature of the Melchizedek Priesthood itself. This Priesthood does not depend on any one human lineage like the Levitical Priesthood. It is of Heaven. Also, we need not spiritualize Shem away and say Jesus met Abram. Hebrews states that Melchizedek was created like unto the Son of God. Jesus was not created but begotten. Shem was an actual man and founder and king of Salem in his day.

There also is a heavenly Melchizedek. Above, there are many orders of created beings beyond the normal ones that we are familiar with such as humans, angels, seraphim and cherubim. Examples are the watchers and the holy ones mentioned in Daniel 4:17. What if Melchizedek is a created being with flesh on him, a kind of prototype of the High Priest of Israel or a type of the Son of God who taught Shem how do be a Melchizedek on earth for a time? Moreover, what if Melchizedek is the Father's High Priest? Some believe that the twenty-four elders represent orders of created beings. The belief is that each elder exists as a prototype or a genesis of individual classes of beings having all different shapes, sizes, powers, and functions.

There Were Two Distinct Groups of Levites

The terms Aaronic and Levitical are sometimes used synonymously, although there are some specific differences in the offices existing within the Levitical Priesthood. For example, the lesser priesthood was conferred only upon men of the tribe of Levi. However, within the tribe, only Aaron and his sons could hold the office of priest. And, still further, from the firstborn of Aaron's sons was selected the high priest. Thus Aaron and his sons after him had greater offices in the Levitical Priesthood than did the other Levites. It is interesting that Aaron was God's mouthpiece in assisting Moses.

The operations of the priests were greater than those who functioned in the other Levitical offices, and a distinction between the two is evident when the scripture speaks of them as "the priests and the Levites" (1 Kgs. 8:4; Ezra 2:70; John 1:19). The priests could burn incense on the altar, offer sacrifices for the people, and teach the law, whereas the other Levites were employed in more domestic tasks, such as the housekeeping of the tabernacle, transporting the Ark of the

Covenant, keeping oil in the lamps, taking down and setting up the tabernacle when moving, and related tasks in assisting the priests (Num. 3:5–10; 18:1–7; 1 Chr. 23:27–32). The Aaronic (or Levitical) Priesthood thus functioned only within the tribe of Levi, and the right to have it conferred upon one was determined by lineage and worthiness. It is important to denote that this book is about the Order of Melchizedek as it relates to the higher functioning High Priest as a modern-day Melchizedek. Melchizedek is also akin to the lower functioning (but still important) priests and this is what Peter describes as the "Royal Priesthood" of all believers. I Peter 2:9 *"But you are a chosen people, a royal priesthood, a holy nation, God's special possession, that you may declare the praises of him who called you out of darkness into his wonderful light."* There is only one Order of Melchizedek as there was only one Order of Levites, however, as there were two classes within the Levites, there are as well with the modern-day expression of The Order. The "normal" Christians who have become enlightened to their role in The Order as well as the executive function, Chief or Principal Melchizedek's that this book addresses. This has been the source of confusion between what I have written and some of the works that have gone before, but now cleared up. To reiterate, *all believers are called* unto the Melchizedek Order but in another way only the Father can call someone in the role of a "High Priest", a Chief or Principal Melchizedek (also called an Elder in this book, or a person in the office of a Melchizedek

Priest) and to minister unto the Father. Even as the brain of a human has an executive function within the Prefrontal Cortex. From Wikipedia *"Executive function relates to abilities to differentiate among conflicting thoughts, determine good and bad, better and best, same and different, future consequences of current activities, working toward a defined goal, prediction of outcomes, expectation based on actions, and social "control" (the ability to suppress urges that, if not suppressed, could lead to socially unacceptable outcomes)"*. So also does The Order, to lead and direct all higher-level "thinking" activities in which The Order is involved. So, too are Yeshua and the Father the executives of The Order itself. It is to this group called into the Holy of Holies, not just once a year but as often as the Father desires that this book is written, but *either* group will benefit from this material. You can benefit if you are hungry to attain to the higher level. Melchizedek as mentioned in this book is written to you as a Principal Melchizedek, an executor in the making. A Levite Priest could never go into the Holy of Holies. Do you want to be there? Ask God and read on...

Treasurer of Heaven

Abraham tithed to Melchizedek. This act is the first time that tithing is mentioned in the Word. Tithing was practiced 400 years before the law was given. Tithing is, in effect, instituted by God. What prompted Abraham to tithe to Melchizedek? The Bible does not say. I asked the Lord about tithing, and He said it was customary to give a gift to a king! Melchizedek was the king of Salem. The Queen of Sheba brought gifts to Solomon. The three wise men brought gifts to Jesus at His birth as they followed the star in the east. Just like I have, some have met Melchizedek in heaven or by an appearance on earth. These say that he is the Treasurer of heaven. I, too, confirm by way of revelation his role as heaven's Treasurer. Seer Shawn Bolz shares the existence of a heavenly treasurer in his *Keys to Heaven's Economy: An Angelic Visitation from the Minister of Finance.* Ian Clayton says, "Melchizedek is the chief chancellor of the treasury room of heaven. The treasury room dispenses the wealth of heaven to the sons of God." Source: http://god-talk.ca/Melchizedek.php. Stay tuned for more revelation in book II.

Needed: Melchizedek Revelation
I asked the Lord why there were so few Scriptures on Melchizedek, and the Lord replied that it's because Melchizedek is an evolving priesthood. By that, He means that our understanding of The Priesthood is evolving or growing every day. There will be many books on Melchizedek in the future. You will be hearing about The Order a lot. Titles addressing healing under The Order of Melchizedek will be forthcoming. Already, marketplace Apostle Francis Myles has written *Breaking Generational Curses Under The Order of Melchizedek: God's Remedy to Generational and Genetic Anomalies* and *Tithing Under The Order of Melchizedek: The Return of the Lost Key.* By the way,

Myles wrote *The Order of Melchizedek: Rediscovering the Eternal Royal Priesthood of Jesus Christ*, a book that broke new ground in 2008.

As for my reading on Melchizedek, I've read chapters in Myles' 2008 book on the Order. However, I have read *Melchizedek the New Millennium Priesthood* by Nita Johnson. Reading Nita Johnson's book started me on my own Melchizedek journey three years ago. Also, I do quote *Back to the Melchizedek Future* by Dr. David L. Perry, a book more geared toward the Jewish mindset.

We can obtain knowledge about The Order through reading these books, through our hunger and thirst after the Lord as Melchizedek Priest, and by ascending and experiencing *"being seated with Him in heavenly places."* (Ephesians 2:6.) We can even meet Melchizedek and be trained personally by the seven Spirits of God if this is what the Father deems necessary for our education. Thus, the way can open to obtain firsthand revelation about this priesthood. (See *Foundations,* Chapter 11: Seeing into Eternity.)

The other priesthoods were given by God to the people, but this priesthood was God's from the beginning and is a part of God. The Melchizedek priesthood is not a type patterned after the Levitical or Zadok priesthoods. (Zadok was another part of Aaron's family.) Instead, the Levitical is patterned after The Order of Melchizedek, the true priesthood. These earthly priesthoods are just a shadow of the true. They were given; the

37

other just IS. It's like the "I AM" name of YHWH. Remember, He, too, has no beginning and no ending. The true priesthood represents the relationship between Father and Son most perfectly. If we can grasp the way they relate, we can grasp The Priesthood. As much as God Himself is a mystery so, too, The Priesthood is a mystery to most. The Priesthood is a mystery except to those whom the Father and Son will to reveal it. Those who are willing to pay the price and come up to higher spiritual heights will ascend the golden staircase of God to reach the lofty heights. (See Song of Songs 2:14 KJV.) Think of Jacob's ladder: *"He dreamed that there was a ladder (stairway) placed on the earth, and the top of it reached [out of sight] toward heaven."* (Genesis 28:12 AMP.) At our first Tipping Point conference in 2012, I saw this ladder. This year, 2015, I've seen multiple steps added signifying that believers can now reach heights like Paul did.

As for my own encounter, Melchizedek stood before me in an open vision in 2015. He was bearded and had on what looked like priestly garments. He exuded holiness and righteousness. *The* Melchizedek carried the presence of one who had been with the Father, one who had been in heaven, and his presence filled the room. As he raised his arms to me, revelation about what The Order really is filled my spirit. And afterward, I wrote what was communicated—some of which is in this book.

The Melchizedek Priesthood has always existed, and like Melchizedek himself, it has no beginning and no ending. It is not a natural creation. Speaking of the king of Salem, the Word says,

Who is Melchizedek?

"Without father, without mother, without descent, having neither beginning of days, nor end of life." (Hebrews 7:3.)

There was no high priest on the earth in Abram's time because the only covenant that existed was between God and Abram. God had not even changed his name to Abraham yet. (Genesis 17:5.) It was 400 years before the law was given. But God preserved Shem, son of Noah, through the flood, and he served as the first Melchizedek Priest. Shem pictured for us Jesus who was to come. God needed someone holy, someone to preserve the purity of heaven's line as it descended from Adam, to Abel, Seth, Enoch the seventh from Adam to Methuselah whose name means "when he is dead, it (the flood) shall come." And the flood did come the year Methuselah died. Methuselah lived 969 years; he was the oldest living person ever recorded and a sign of God's longsuffering. Noah followed him. Shem and Abram were contemporaries.

Shem was the actual king of Salem. He was a marketplace man. But he also functioned as a priest. Now, the Father's High Priest in heaven was and is Melchizedek. Melchizedek in heaven taught Shem, the first Melchizedek on earth, just as he is appearing to teach us. The Bible does not call him Shem. Genesis 14:8 calls him, *"Melchizedek king of Salem."* Remember, God loves to change names. Thus we can call ourselves Melchizedek or kings of righteousness. Who are you, again? You are not Tom, Dick or Harry—you are now Melchizedek. I predict that a lot of boys will be named Melchizedek in the future. Parents will call their sons "Mel."

In heaven, Yeshua is the head of the Order. Melchizedek, who is a created being, but not an angel, exists with Him in heaven. He has flesh and bone and functions as the prototype and trainer of all Melchizedek's to follow. Could Melchizedek be a holy one? I note that Psalm 89 refers to a *"council of the holy ones."*

Melchizedek: the Hidden Wisdom of God

Unlocking the Mysteries

Consider 1 Corinthians 2:6-14:

> *Yet we do speak wisdom among those who are mature; a wisdom, however, not of this age nor of the rulers of this age, who are passing away; but we speak God's wisdom in a mystery, the hidden wisdom which God predestined before the ages to our glory the wisdom which none of the rulers of this age has understood; for if they had understood it they would not have crucified the Lord of glory; but just as it is written, "THINGS WHICH EYE HAS NOT SEEN AND EAR HAS NOT HEARD, AND WHICH HAVE NOT ENTERED THE HEART OF MAN, ALL THAT GOD HAS PREPARED FOR THOSE WHO LOVE HIM." For to us God revealed them through the Spirit; for the Spirit searches all things, even*

the depths of God. For who among men knows the thoughts of a man except the spirit of the man which is in him? Even so the thoughts of God no one knows except the Spirit of God. Now we have received, not the spirit of the world, but the Spirit who is from God, so that we may know the things freely given to us by God, which things we also speak, not in words taught by human wisdom, but in those taught by the Spirit, combining spiritual thoughts with spiritual words. But a natural man does not accept the things of the Spirit of God, for they are foolishness to him; and he cannot understand them, because they are spiritually appraised.

The Order is here to unlock the hidden wisdom and the mysteries that can only be found in the heights of heaven. In New Testament times, the Apostle Paul operated in the level of revelation that The Priesthood will be operating in. I believe Paul wrote Hebrews including the passages of Hebrews 5, 6, and 7 on Melchizedek from his rapture into the third heaven where he heard and saw much of the revelation for his New Testament letters. Likely Paul saw the heavenly Priesthood in operation. Paul records being caught up to heaven in 2 Corinthians 12:1-7.

Boasting is necessary, though it is not profitable; but I will go on to visions and revelations of the Lord. I know a man in Yeshua who fourteen years ago—whether in the body I do not know, or out of the body I do not know, God knows—such a man was caught up to the third heaven. And I know how such a man—whether in the body or apart from the body I do not know, God knows was caught up into Paradise and heard inexpressible words, which a man is not permitted to speak. On behalf of such a man I will boast; but on my own behalf I will not boast, except in regard to my weaknesses. For if I do wish to boast I will not be foolish, for I will be speaking the truth; but I refrain from this, so that no one will credit me with more than he sees in me or hears from me. Because of the surpassing greatness of the revelations, for this reason, to keep me from exalting myself, there was given me a thorn in the flesh, a messenger of Satan to torment me— to keep me from exalting myself!

2 Corinthians was written by Paul in AD 55. Hebrews was written around AD 63-64. So Paul wrote Hebrews eight years after he wrote 2 Corinthians. In 2 Corinthians, the apostle discusses being caught up to the third heaven in approximately AD 41. (Written in AD 55. 14 years ago caught up.) Could he have seen Melchizedek discharging his priestly duties? Was what Paul saw the basis of the *"better priesthood"* passage in Hebrews 7? Could the revelation of Melchizedek in Hebrews, the most eloquently written book of the New Testament, be related to Paul's catching away 14 years prior and hearing *"inexpressible words, which a man is not permitted to speak"*? I believe that even if Paul did not pen Hebrews he knew of this

Who is Melchizedek?

writing and approved of it. Perhaps Priscilla wrote it. My point is that Paul did not have to be the author for there to be a valid relationship from Paul's catching up recorded in 2 Corinthians 12 to the New Testament Melchizedek references found in Hebrews, 5, 6, and 7.

Paul writes of having surpassing great revelations of the Lord and likely while in heaven of his eternal priesthood. So he, or an author familiar with Paul's rapture, declares in Hebrews 7:26, "For such an high priest became us, who is holy, harmless, undefiled, separate from sinners, and made higher than the heavens." From Hebrews 8:4-12, we get the description of the heavenly realities and the better Melchizedek system of heaven under which we are all invited in.

> *Now if he were still living on earth he would not be a priest at all, for there are already priests offering the gifts prescribed by the Law. These men are serving what is only a pattern or reproduction of things that exist in heaven. (Moses, you will remember, when he was going to construct the tabernacle, was cautioned by God in these words: 'See that you make all things according to the pattern shown you on the mountain'.) But Yeshua had been given a far higher ministry for he mediates a higher agreement, which in turn rests upon higher promises. If the first agreement had proved satisfactory there would have been no need for the second. Actually, however, God does show himself dissatisfied for he says to those under the first*

agreement: 'Behold, the days are coming, says the Lord, when I will make a new covenant with the house of Israel and with the house of Judah—not according to the covenant that I made with their fathers in the day when I took them by the hand to lead them out of the land of Egypt; because they did not continue in my covenant, and I disregarded them, says the Lord. For this is the covenant that I will make with the house of Israel: After those days, says the Lord, I will put my laws in their mind and write them on their hearts; and I will be their God, and they shall be my people. None of them shall teach his neighbour, and none his brother, saying, Know the Lord, for all shall know me, from the least to the greatest of them. For I will be merciful to their unrighteousness, and their sins and their lawless deeds I will remember no more.'

Melchizedek and Mysticism

It's easy to become mystical over Melchizedek as many New Agers and Mormons have done in seeking Melchizedek. The need is to discern the false mysticism from the true. There is a mystery surrounding his sudden, kingly appearance. He showed up right after Abram defeated the kings with the king of Sodom about to destroy him and offered Abram the table of the Lord. Then there is the way he seemed to transcend the times of Abraham as if he came from another world. Reverential awe was about him as founder of perhaps the first city for God,

Salem[1], which later became Jerusalem. And there is the mystical in the truth that a reference to Melchizedek really means a reference to Yeshua. It's otherworldly that Melchizedek could have taught the actual king Shem the precepts of El Elyon, The Most High God of heaven. And, too, there is the Melchizedek Order under the God of heaven

I believe the heavenly Melchizedek *is* a holy one, one of a higher order of beings than angels who are similar to humans in appearance. Daniel 8:12-13 uses the title holy one.

> *And on account of transgression the host will be given over to the horn along with the regular sacrifice; and it will fling truth to the ground and perform its will and prosper. Then I heard a holy one speaking, and another holy one said to that particular one who was speaking," How long will the vision about the regular sacrifice apply, while the transgression causes horror, so as to allow both the holy place and the host to be trampled?"*

The Dead Sea Scrolls Identify
Melchizedek is mentioned in the first century Dead Sea Scrolls 11 times. I know after studying the Dead Sea Scrolls that The Order is one of Paul's greatest revelations. It ranks up there with grace. (For more on the Scrolls and Melchizedek, see *Foundations* Chapter 13: Resources: The Meat of Melchizedek.)

---

[1] Shem was the founder of Salem according to Jewish scholars.

Additionally, 7th and 9th century references to those that call themselves Melchizedek's as the "untouchables" can be found in https://en.wikipedia.org/wiki/Athinganoi
The *Athinganoi* or *Athingani*, Ancient Greek: Ἀθίγγανοι, plural of **Athinganos** (Ἀθίγγανος), were a 9th-century sect of Monarchians located in Phrygia, founded by Theodotus the banker. The etymology of the word is not certain, but a common determination is a derivation in Greek for "(the) untouchables" derived from a privative alpha prefix and the verb *thingano* (Θιγγάνω, to touch). It is uncertain whether the sect survived beyond the 9th century. They were probably scattered across Anatolia and the Balkans following the destruction of the Paulician capital Tephrike in the 870s.

An earlier, and probably quite distinct, sect with the same name is refuted by Marcus Eremita, who seems to have been a disciple of St. John Chrysostom. His book *Eis ton Melchisedek*, or according to Photius "Against the Melchisedekites",[1] speaks of these new teachers as making Melchisedech an incarnation of the Logos (divine Word). They were anathematized by the bishops, but would not cease to preach. They seem to have been otherwise orthodox. St. Jerome (Ep. 73) refutes an anonymous work which identified Melchisedech with the Holy Ghost. About AD 600, Timotheus, Presbyter of Constantinople, in his book *De receptione Haereticorum* [2] adds at the end of his list of heretics who need rebaptism the Melchisedechians, "now called *Athingani*. They live in Phrygia, and are neither Hebrews nor Gentiles. They keep the Sabbath, but are not circumcised. They will not touch any man. If food is offered to them, they ask for it to be placed on the ground; then they come and take it. They give to others with the same precautions."

Chapter 3: Melchizedek Transformation

Abrahamic Encounter

It takes just one Abrahamic encounter with Melchizedek to transform a man or woman. What did encounter with the king-priest Melchizedek do for Abram?

Establishment in God

First, it established him. Abram had at the time a relationship with God that went up to a point. (Please review Abram's encounters with God up to and including his meeting with Melchizedek in Genesis.) However, Abram did not really know the attributes of the Son of God; he didn't know that the bread and the wine offered him by Melchizedek stood for Jesus' body and blood to be shed thousands of years later. Abram did not have the peace of God as he needed. Melchizedek was a peacemaker as the king and founder of Salem, which means peace. And he was a type or shadow of the coming Prince of Peace, Jesus. Abram did not know how to minister before the Lord as Melchizedek did—God's priest or representative in that day. He did not have the kingly nature of Melchizedek, the statesman's diplomatic nature, or perhaps even the business/trade and entrepreneurial abilities of Melchizedek. Abram did not have a relationship with God like the steward and the emissary of heaven on earth, Melchizedek. He had not experienced the holiness of God as Melchizedek had. Abram had faith and God *"accounted it to him for righteousness"*

(Galatians 3:6), but he himself did not have the righteousness of God. Melchizedek imparted to him all these needed things in the holy meal when he communed with him as recorded in Genesis 14. While Abram communed with Melchizedek, God the Father and God the Son were present. The founder of the holy city ministered and equipped Abram in God. There well may have been subsequent encounters between Abram and Melchizedek though the Bible is silent on this.

Therefore, just as in this example of Melchizedek impartation to Abram, God will use us of The Order to establish YHWH's people in these same things. Do go back and reread the above on Abram and Melchizedek, and see yourself as Melchizedek imparting unto God's choice servants everything that Melchizedek imparted to Abram. See yourself receiving these very qualities from God Himself. Ask God to meet you as Melchizedek if you have not already. My experience is that the Melchizedek in heaven radiates the same qualities that we see in the Melchizedek of Genesis 14. We can also receive these qualities from Yeshua, but I note that these qualities are the qualities of the Father and the Son *as exemplified through Melchizedek.*

Blessing
Second, this encounter blessed Abram. Melchizedek blessed him in the name of the Most High God. Abram needed what author Sandie Freed calls a "destiny link" on the earth to establish his

goings and bless his path. God, Himself, ordained The Priesthood to provide such an access to God's holiness and the blessings and benefits thereof. God must have told Melchizedek that this man Abram was special and that he was going to represent His name in the earth. Likely Melchizedek knew that God had set him apart and called him away from his family in Ur of the Chaldees for a special work and assignment. Hebrews 7:6 tells us Melchizedek *"blessed him that had the promises."* Without Melchizedek's blessing, Abram would not have been able to fulfill God's promises for him including his plans to make the numbers of Abram's children *"as the stars of the heaven, and as the sand which is upon the sea shore."* (Genesis 22:17.) It was when Abram tithed to Melchizedek that he received the blessings of multiplication and its fruit in his life. As he tithed to God's representative on the earth, this act settled his fortune. This one tithe offering provided the future means for Abram's seed as if his seed had tithed unto this priest. The Scripture says of Levi that he, *"payed tithes in Abraham. For he was yet in the loins of his father, when Melchisedec met him."* (Hebrews 7:9-10 KJV.)

God removed a ceiling on Abram's life when he tithed unto Melchizedek and partook of the symbolic meal of bread and wine. A sacrifice of finances goes together with the sacrifice of the Lamb. You cannot have blessing without dedicating the tenth. If God is raising you up as a Priest in this Order, tell your people that the same blessing of multiplication and fruitfulness that came to Abram when he tithed is over them when they tithe to you. Let the Lord lead you and your people in this, but Melchizedek's example of receiving a tenth of all applies to us as well. Claim your financial blessing as a potential Priest in our Order. Go over this section on tithing again and see yourself as a Priest in The Order blessing those whom God causes you to encounter.

From Hebrews 7:4-7, we see the revelation of The Order as the greater priesthood. Verse 7 emphasizes that *"the lessor is blessed by the greater."*

> *Now observe how great this man was to whom Abraham, the patriarch, gave a tenth of the choicest spoils. And those indeed of the sons of Levi who receive the priest's office have commandment in the Law to collect a tenth from the people, that is, from their brethren, although these are descended from Abraham. But the one whose genealogy is not traced from them collected a tenth from Abraham and blessed the one who had the promises. And without doubt the lesser is blessed by the greater.*

Melchizedek was not of the tribe of Levi, yet he received tithes from Abram. Remember, the Levitical system had not been instituted yet. It was but a shadow of The Order as we have learned. Abram needed the blessing of Melchizedek. There was something about the powerful combination of king and priest, his rule of Salem, his relationship with God as the priest of the

Most High. Melchizedek had something that Abram needed. An anointing, a blessing. The world and especially the church are going to need what we of The Order have. They will need the blessing of our God, both financially and personally. They will need the deeper and higher communion with God and someone to show them the way into this. The Priesthood will show the church the way and call them to come up much higher in the spirit. All need to partake of the bread and the wine, the body and blood of Yeshua. Genesis 14:18 records, *"Then Melchizedek king of Salem brought out bread and wine. He was priest of God Most High."*

Note the way Melchizedek both blessed Abram *and* led him into a new level of communion with God. So shall it be for The Priesthood. In a foreshadowing of The Last Supper, Melchizedek invited Abram into this covenantal relationship with YHWH. Abram was invited even then to partake of the body and blood of Yeshua. I believe Shem as Melchizedek was known for acts of blessing. This practice helped him make peace with his adversaries and enter into covenantal relationships with other kings and leaders. Salem stayed in a peaceful state with those around her. Wherever Melchizedek went, he made peace with those against him. However, though he had God with him, his appearance was not a "Christophany" or the pre-incarnate Yeshua on earth. He was a real man who was the king of Salem. Perhaps he served as the only ambassador of the kingdom of God in that day, a forerunner of the coming King of kings. God

53

always has at least one person in every age who calls on His name and serves Him.

Change of Name Change of Nature

Third, the encounter qualified Abram to receive God's act to change his name. In the Bible, a change of someone's name indicates a new walk or often a new assignment with new responsibilities. A name change comes with honor. After changing Abram's name to Abraham, God changed Jacob's name to Israel. Prophetic of a real nature change, name change has to do with God's assignment. Abram means "Exalted Father." Abraham means "Father of a Multitude." If Abram had never identified with the body and blood of Yeshua through eating and drinking the priest's bread and wine, he would not have gotten a new name—God's new name for him. In some way, he was saved through the death, burial and resurrection of the Lamb. If he had not honored God's representative on the earth as a figure of Yeshua, the ONLY ONE who fully bore God's name in all of earth's history, he would have gotten a name change but it would have been "mud." Dirt. Having God the Father, Himself, change your name is like having God adopt you as His own.

Seriously, Abram had passed God's tests in the Melchizedek meeting. He still had some character issues as he lied to Pharaoh and to a king saying Sarah was his sister. God knows we are but dust, and He forgives. But Abram's dealing with the king of

Salem was right in line with what God wanted. God was watching as Abram met this living, breathing emissary and priest of El Elyon. How did Abram know to give a tenth of the spoils to Melchizedek? Abram knew that God was with him in the battle of the nine kings that it was God who had spared his life and the lives of his servants. Certainly Abram was grateful to God for these victories. Abram was obviously a warrior. I do not think Melchizedek asked him for a tenth. Instead, either God spoke to Abram directly or the kingly, priestly, and holy presence upon Melchizedek emanating the very glory of God convinced Abram. It's as if Abram said, "I have never met such a man like this. He is almost a God, and I want to be like him. I want to know God like him. And I have got to have what he has!" So, too, will this happen when people meet us as Melchizedek. You need to see that part of the Melchizedek blessing is finances. God's plan is for each Priest to be able to fulfill his or her mandate from God and to issue support. We will be flying at such a high altitude with God in this. Are you ready to change people's lives as a Melchizedek Priest? See yourself blessing many Abram's financially. You are going to impact people in this same way. Let these principles sink in. I am blessing you in this way by this book. Read and absorb this material. You will want to reread sections periodically to let their truths sink in. This material gives you the next step in the stairway to heaven so to speak.

The Apostle Paul said, *"Be ye followers of me, even as I also am of Yeshua."* (1 Corinthians 11:1 KJV.) As Melchizedek, you will have followers, and you will impact them in all these ways and more. God is going to change your name and your followers' names. As prophesied by the Lord in Revelation 2:17 KJV, *"To him that overcometh will I give . . . a white stone, and in the stone a new name written, which no man knoweth saving he that receiveth it."* Years ago in a visitation, the Lord said "the New Jerusalem" in relation to my new name. I believe it's by our new names that we will have access into the heavenly city coming down. God is giving individuals a new start and a new direction in Him. Many cannot fulfill their callings without you coming forth as Melchizedek. You may not be able to fulfill your calling without this book. Read on. Let these sections on Melchizedek encounter sink in. They may prove to be your greatest takeaways from this how-to manual!

Summary of Abram's Encounter

Abram's response to Melchizedek needs to be your response and my response to God as He introduces us to The Priesthood through an *encounter* with this book! Yes, if you are open and receptive you *will* encounter God through this book! I promise! The anointing on it is very tangible right now as I write it here in my apartment in China. This book was entirely written in China, in Asia. There alone with God, He revealed Himself to me as Abba in a profound way. He helped me see into coming days.

I recommend that you *"ponder these things in your heart"* like Mary did after receiving the message from the angel that she would give birth to the Yeshua. (Luke 2:19.) Consider taking communion before going on as this is a holy time before God and His calling. You are being changed. You are even now being transfigured.

Melchizedek Transfiguration

Friend, now is the time we must encounter Father God. There is no more time left for delays and excuses. Either, I plead, move forward with me or get out of the way. I am tired of church as usual. Powerless Christianity. We need to create a new model for how we do church meetings, and how we spend our time together. We need both efficiency and effectiveness. Efficiency is needed to optimize resources such as time, money and personnel. We need to measure effectiveness by each answering the question, "Am I achieving my goals?" God is efficient. And God has goals. He is effective, and He has a timeline for bringing forth The Order. (See *Foundations*, Chapter 6: School for Melchizedek's on seven-year initial time frame for God's training.) We should ask ourselves after every service, "Did going to church today further prepare me for my calling?"

How do we encounter God? We encounter God, first, by being willing to wait on Him and then actually giving time to wait on Him. As a potential Melchizedek Priest you must have the commissioning of the Father. He must visit you in a tangible way and speak to you and show you your role as Melchizedek.

Jesus' Transfiguration

Traditional priests had to be from the DNA of Aaron. God's new and better way is for His line of saints to receive *His own DNA*. I heard that in Israel they found blood stains that had DNA from only one of the parents i.e. the DNA from the Father was missing. Could this be Yeshua's blood? Red blood cells do not carry a copy of our DNA. White blood cells, however, do carry a copy of our DNA. If that spilled blood had white cells in it or even some flesh cells then the DNA could be tested. According to FamilyTreeDNA's post on "Understanding DNA":

> At conception, a person receives DNA from both the father and mother. Each human has 23 pairs of chromosomes. Of each pair, one was received from the Father, and one was received from the mother. These 23 pairs of chromosomes are known as nuclear DNA because, with the exception of red blood cells, they reside in the nucleus of every cell in the body. The 23rd chromosome is known as the sex chromosome. As with the other chromosomes, one is inherited from the Father,

and one from the mother. The 23rd chromosome from the mother is always an X. From the Father, a person either inherits an X chromosome or a Y chromosome. The chromosome inherited from the Father determines their gender. An X from the Father would result in an XX combination, which is a female. A Y from the Father would result in an XY combination, which is a male.

The Holy Spirit determined the XY male gender for Yeshua as Mary became *"pregnant—by the Holy Spirit."* (Matthew 1:18 PHILLIPS.) But did the Holy Spirit provide the needed 23 chromosomes as well? I think the Spirit had to for Jesus to be able to live.

Both parents contribute to the DNA that is found in every cell other than the red blood cells of every human being. Jesus had human DNA by Mary, His mother, which means that the Savior as God had to work through a human nature. He had to overcome the limitations of being a man. Hebrews 4:15 PHILLIPS puts it well: *"For we have no superhuman High Priest to whom our weaknesses are unintelligible—he himself has shared fully in all our experience of temptation, except that he never sinned."*

On the high mountain, Jesus came into a glorified state. The Father, Himself, overshadowed Jesus: *"a light-radiant cloud enveloped them, and sounding from deep in the cloud a voice: "This is my Son, marked by my love, focus of my delight. Listen to him."* (Matthew 17:5 The Message.) What happened to Jesus' human

DNA there? Let's just say the Father completed it when he became transfigured as light. On that mountain, Jesus was as Melchizedek, having not only no earthly Father but also in a sense no earthly mother. Though Jesus still had to conquer Gethsemane and the cross as an anointed man, in the Father's impartation Jesus was changed in a way that prefigured a glory available to The Order. Jesus was in the eternal realm. Like Melchizedek, *"He had no father or mother and no family tree. He was not born nor did he die."* (Hebrews 7:3 PHILLIPS.) Jesus Christ was and is, *"A priest forever according to The Order of Melchizedek."* (Hebrews 5:6 PHILLIPS.) Hallelujah!

In Melchizedek glory, we have the potential to overcome our very DNA. The Bible refers to the changed state coming to believers in two places. Paul said in 1 Corinthians 15:51-53, *"Listen, and I will tell you a secret. We shall not all die, but suddenly, in the twinkling of an eye, every one of us will be changed as the trumpet sounds! The trumpet will sound and the dead shall be raised beyond the reach of corruption, and we who are still alive shall suddenly be utterly changed. For this perishable nature of ours must be wrapped in imperishability, these bodies which are mortal must be wrapped in immortality.* As the coming of the kingdom is progressive, we as Melchizedek can enter into levels of this glorious transformation now. The change referred to here is not necessarily the "rapture" but a Melchizedek re-synching or transfiguration. On the mount, the Father was saying here is the apostolic (Moses) and the prophetic office (Elijah) combining with The Order of Melchizedek functions of Jesus—High Priest and King of kings and Lord of lords. What if such a transformation will happen to people of The Order first and then they lead the way for the rest of the Body? What if we reach immortality and do the greatest works of all time? 1 John 3:2 could happen now: *"Beloved, now are we the sons of God, and it doth not yet appear what we shall be: but we know that, when he shall appear, we shall be like him; for we shall see him as he is."* Let us ponder this.

The Face of the Father

Have you had *your* encounter with Melchizedek and ultimately the Father? Meeting the Father is, of course, a much greater honor as you can imagine. When you do encounter God the Father, I guarantee that you will fall on your knees as I did in awe of His excellence. He is indescribable really. Seek these experiences. Hunger after them. If you are hungry for such *"meat in due season,"* God will certainly provide it for you. (Psalm 104:27.) This is the Father's time, and it's His age. It is essential to find Him as He wants to communicate with you, His Melchizedek Priest. Moses asked God to show him His face. Isn't that what we all want? To see our Father's face and experience His smile upon us? His most excellent smile? The face of God *will change you* like it changed and qualified Abram and like it changed me. I certainly have not "arrived" just because I've been commissioned by the Father to write this book. If anything, it's just that I have been faithful and obedient to Him in the past. And my obedience is why he chose me. God did tell me through a prophet's word years ago that I was one of His favorite messengers. What can I say in response to such favor? I can only say, "thank you, Father." "I am here because of You and all glory belongs to You." Hopefully, there will be many other excellent books on face-to-face intimate encounters with Abba. As we look at Him ... we are all changed. Transformed. *"But all of us who are Christians have no veils on our faces, but reflect like mirrors the glory of the Lord. We are transfigured by the Spirit of the Lord in ever-increasing splendour into His own image."* (2 Corinthians 3:18 PHILLIPS.)

Right now the Father is in the earth. He is seeking men and women to be a host company for Him in the Order. As I write these pages, I am in China ministering to souls and advising several companies. God the Father visited me here. He came to me in a way I had never before experienced. In seeing Him and the smoky cloud of His holy presence, I instantly fell to my knees. He spoke, "As I was with Moses, I will be with you. And as I was with Joseph, I will be with you." I noted that both Moses and Joseph lived as foreigners in foreign lands. God was with them. In China, God was with me. Then He said, "I want you, as a Melchizedek Priest, to anoint the leaders of the conglomerate." So, God, Himself called me a Melchizedek. Previously He had called me a "Joseph" in China. And though I've completed only three of the seven years required training for The Order, in God's eyes I am a Melchizedek. I did anoint two leaders of the conglomerate—myself and another man. I had never anointed myself, but God said to do so. The others were not ready. I continue to wait on God for all that is ahead. So firsthand I've experienced an out-of-the-box Father God. He is free to move on the earth in vessels or boxes like me as we contain Him, our impenetrable fortress within. Wherever I go in China, I take Him.

The Father is higher than the Son. They are not coequals, Jesus stated in John 14, *"the Father is greater than I."* However, Father, Son, and Holy Spirit are all God. Scripture proves this. The Father begot or birthed the Son from Himself so who was first? Being begotten detracts nothing from the Son as God. Actually Jesus as the only begotten of God gives the Father that honor that is due Him by declaring Him. *"No man hath seen God at any time, the only begotten Son, which is in the bosom of the Father, he hath declared him."* (John 1:18 KJV.) The Son agrees by His own words.

Chapter 4: The Melchizedek Priesthood

Yeshua's Own Order

The Order of Melchizedek is Yeshua's own order. Yeshua was not from the tribe of Levi, and neither are most of us. Therefore, we are not eligible to be Levitical priests. However, all who will *are* called to be Melchizedek priests. In this sense all believers from *"every kindred, and tongue, and people, and nation"* have the opportunity to be in the Priesthood. (Revelation 5:9.) ((Source: Perry, Dr. David. 2013. *Back to the Melchizedek Future.* Raleigh: Lulu.)

Melchizedek cannot be romanced and glorified above Yeshua Himself. The Order is His priesthood. But it can never replace Him for He is the head of the Body, and the Melchizedek Order is a part of Him. Without Yeshua, there is no Melchizedek Priesthood. Again, His death, burial, resurrection, and ascension made the way for the very priesthood we aspire to. Note that the name Melchizedek refers both to Yeshua and His Order.

Think about the uniqueness of this Order under Yeshua. What other orders or ordinances has Yeshua initiated? The Lord's Supper, a sacred ceremony. Check. Whom are Yeshua's own people? Those that He died for. Check. Who administers Yeshua's own government? The Melchizedek Order does. I did not say what but who. The Priesthood is about a people, the ruling class of heaven on earth. But, remember, to be above all means to serve all. The Order works this way: *"No, whoever among you wants to be great must become the servant of you all, and if he wants to be first among you he must be the slave of all men! For the Son of Man himself has not come to be served but to serve, and to give His life to set many others free."* (Mark 10:44 PHILLIPS.)

I desire that all Jews go back to their Hebraic roots vs. their rabbinic/Jewish roots. Also, I also instruct Christians to learn the Hebraic roots of their faith.

Yeshua the Pattern Melchizedek Priest

The Levitical priesthood was at its very best damage control or God's Plan B according to Dr. David Perry in his book, *Back to the Melchizedek Future*. Instituting the Levitical order was a second string solution—a scramble to regroup under the Levites granted by YHWH to divert Him from a mass genocide of the Israelites—His judgment against Israel's idolatrous golden calf worship. It makes perfect sense that Yeshua would be protected from ever being a part of a less than perfect or second best priesthood. The Melchizedek Priesthood was never an option for any Israelite of any tribe until after Yeshua's death, resurrection, and ascension.

The perfect and eternal nature of Yeshua's Melchizedek Priesthood is set forth for us in Hebrews 8:3-6. No need any longer for any inferior setup.

> *For every high priest is appointed to offer both gifts and sacrifices; so it is necessary that this high priest also have*

65

something to offer. Now if He were on earth, He would not be a priest at all, since there are those who offer the gifts according to the Law; who serve a copy and shadow of the heavenly things, just as Moses was warned by God when he was about to erect the tabernacle; for, "See," He says, "THAT YOU MAKE ALL THINGS ACCORDING TO THE PATTERN WHICH WAS SHOWN YOU ON THE MOUNTAIN." But now He has obtained a more excellent ministry, by as much as He is also the mediator of a better covenant, which has been enacted on better promises.

To my Jewish and Messianic Christian readers, there is nothing more "Messianic" than the restoration of the original Melchizedek Priesthood under Yeshua, *"the High Priest after The Order of Melchizedek"* of Hebrews 6:20. As a personal observation, it makes sense that if there is going to be an order of High Priests, then there would have to be lower ranking priests under the higher ones. (Source: Perry, Dr. David. 2013. *Back to the Melchizedek Future.* Raleigh: Lulu.)

Moses: a Melchizedek Before Yeshua

Aaron and all the Egypt-Exodus-Israelites had defiled themselves because of their golden calf worship and breach of covenant with Yahweh. Moses, though, walked in the purity of a Melchizedek. He was the last Melchizedek Priesthood priest and mediator until the death and resurrection of Yeshua. Through His death, Yeshua ended the system of ritual laws for Israel. As the risen Lord, He could function as the Melchizedek High Priest that He is. Our place in Yeshua's death and rise to life again[2] also releases us to be Melchizedek Priests in keeping with the original calling of the priests in Exodus but now in the way of life in Yeshua, not in the way of ritual. God is into Plan A again: priests like Melchizedek. (Source: Perry, Dr. David. 2013. *Back to the Melchizedek Future.* Raleigh: Lulu.)

Priests, Prophets, Apostles, *and* Kings

It's important to understand Moses' functions further. Moses was a type of the apostle in the Old Testament as well as a prophet. However, as of yet no modern-day apostle or prophet is operating in the power and authority that Moses operated in. Think about this. Who has turned a rod into a snake or parted a Red Sea today? But when The Order of Melchizedek is released in its full functioning, its priests; who will also be prophets, apostles, and kings; will move in a greater level of power and authority than even Moses did. All four functions will be manifest in each Melchizedek.

The Melchizedek priests will literally operate and host the Spirit of Yeshua Himself in humility and absolute obedience

---

[2] See Romans 6, 7, and 8 on our inclusion in Yeshua's death on the cross and rise to new life.

within their being. By His omnipresence, Yeshua will fill hundreds if not thousands of these leaders, men and women of the four mighty functions of kings, priests, apostles, and prophets. Most importantly, Melchizedek will lead the Body of Yeshua and call the Christian multitudes to great heights in God. They will be examples for all to follow. As Yeshua was to the multitudes who followed Him around Israel, so a multitude of priests will be to the world.

What will follow is a level of unprecedented power and authority as Yeshua Himself fills the earth through His Body. We can expect Habakkuk 2:14 AMP: *"But [the time is coming when] the earth shall be filled with the knowledge of the glory of the Lord, As the waters cover the sea."*

Melchizedek Evolution

The current apostolic and prophetic movements as they are today are the stepping stones to the development and leadership of The Order. Some Christians may start from scratch and be initiated into The Order right after they are saved and filled with Holy Spirit. What better book is there to give to a new convert than this one! By reading it, the new Christian can enter in to the present truths of God even though he is a novice. Others of you may have been operating as apostles or prophets or preferably both and will find yourselves being promoted into The Order like I did.

Requirements for The Priesthood

Melchizedek Priests will uphold:

- The Appointed Times
- Weekly Feast Day and Annual Feast Days
- The Ten Commandments (Exodus 20)
- Accept and Promote Yeshua as Savior and Lord (Romans 10:9)
- Receive the Baptism in the Holy Spirit (Acts 19:2)
- Walk Holy and Blameless before YHWH
- Fellowship with Holy Spirit (2 Corinthians 13:14)
- Promote The Order
- Be pronounced a Melchizedek Priest by the Father directly
- Prophesy and Operate in the Gifts of the Holy Spirit
- Love God's people.

Also, Melchizedek Priests will be living epistles of such passages like Psalm 15 AMP, a Melchizedek Psalm. They will fully walk to the height of the Word of God.

Description of a Citizen of Zion. A Psalm of David.

O Lord, who may lodge [as a guest] in Your tent? Who may dwell [continually] on Your holy hill? He who walks with integrity and strength of character, and works righteousness, And speaks and holds truth in his heart. He does not slander with his tongue, Nor does evil to his neighbor, Nor takes up a reproach against his friend; In his eyes an evil person is despised, But he honors those who fear the Lord [and obediently worship Him with awe-inspired reverence and submissive wonder]. He keeps his word even to his own disadvantage and does not change it [for his own benefit]; He does not put out his money at interest [to a fellow Israelite], And does not take a bribe against the innocent. He who does these things will never be shaken.

Certain attributes mark the Priests of the Melchizedek Order. I list them according to their priority. (For more on these attributes, see *Becoming Melchizedek Book II, Unto Fullness,* Chapter 2: Advanced Training.)

1. Righteousness
2. Humility
3. Holiness
4. Fear of the Lord
5. Counsel
6. Leadership
7. Boldness
8. Servanthood
9. Knowledge of the Word
10. Wisdom
11. Speaking Ability—a great help

The Heavenly Garments

Word of the Lord: I Will Clothe My Melchizedek's

Nita Johnson has said, "Yeshua Himself has a white robe and a golden sash." The garments, says the Lord, will be based upon` the function at hand. There are many wardrobes that I will clothe my Melchizedek Priests in. Just as the Son is seen with His robe dipped in blood. . . .

> *Revelation 19:11-13 I saw heaven standing open and there before me was a white horse, whose rider is called Faithful and True. With justice He judges and wages war. His eyes are like blazing fire, and on His head are many crowns. He has a name written on Him that no one knows but He Himself. He is dressed in a robe dipped in blood, and His name is the Word of God. The armies of heaven were following Him, riding on white horses and dressed in fine linen, white and clean.*

Notice how we are in white linen and Jesus is dressed in a bloody robe. He is a God of war. *The Lord says, the heavenly garments will descend and be given to you. The enemy will not be able to see you but only the garments that you wear—they provide protection and offensive weaponry.* They are similar to the whole armor of God from Ephesians 6. Spiritual garments were worn by Joseph. He wore not just his coat of many colors but his spiritual dress. Moses, the deliverer, wore spiritual garments or mantles in God. Daniel wore them. Elijah wore a mantle as he stood against the 850 prophets of Baal and Asherah. All were clothed in the garments of heaven for their divine assignments, and all were protected. Some spiritual garments actually blind the enemy they shine so brightly. *When my Son was transfigured such that He shone like the brightness of the sun, it was there that I placed a mantle of light upon Him, says the Lord.*

God is Activating Leaders

Today, God is activating The Order of Melchizedek in the lives of many leaders. With this activation comes a new level of wisdom, power, authority, and discernment even over that provided by each of the New Testament five-fold governing offices. Happening is a synergy and a force-multiplication (a military term) between the four faces or sides of Yeshua as they map to God's mantles of king, priest, prophet, and apostle. And all the mantles are now open to each Melchizedek priest-leader. Matthew portrays Yeshua as a king or lion. Mark writes of Him as the ox or strong burden bearer. Luke sees Him as the man-Savior. And John reveals His eagle face—Jesus with the transcendent, powerful life of God. We, as Melchizedek, are moving into the multidimensional in God—all four faces and all mantles.

From Ezekiel 1:10, the four living creatures also have the four faces of Yeshua. These cherubim of Ezekiel looked human, but they had four wings, could move in any direction, and could see for 360 degrees. These creatures differ from the seraphim which actually fly and have six wings. So also can Yeshua's Melchizedek Priesthood see and move freely in the spirit realm.

Again, a Melchizedek can operate in all mantles or capacities combined. When God needs it, you will operate as a prophet. Other times you will operate as an apostle. More frequently you will function as a priest or king. As now you can prophesy at any time as a prophet or just walk into a city as an apostle and have the enemy principalities recognize you instantly, but these offices are being raised to a higher level of accuracy, authority, and power in The Order. Still true, of course, is Amos 3:7, *"Surely the Sovereign LORD does nothing without revealing His plan to His servants the prophets."* Do you see that the expression of God is not complete without its fullness in man?

I have been in preparation for these levels all my life as 20 years ago God called me as a prophet and ten years ago as an apostle. Then it was somewhat unusual for an individual to operate in both Ephesians 4 offices. At times, this dual call caused some confusion for me since people thought you were either an apostle or a prophet with their very different job descriptions and their very different personality styles. To operate in my calling with WISE, I *had* to operate as both prophet and apostle to deal with satanic principalities and powers (Ephesians 6:12) as well as handle deliverance/inner healing ministries as well as prophesy vision for both WISE Ministries and the business leaders from the 100-plus companies that we help.

Also, I have operated as a priest, specifically as a church pastor for five years with my wife Liz in Austin, Texas. And I have been in a kingly role as a corporate pastor/spiritual/executive coach for about 10 years through WISE Ministries. A corporate pastor is a pastor who assists company leadership and company employees for different enterprises. Finally, I have operated as the CEO of four or five for-profit companies. (From coachmybusiness.com, get my manual, *Let Heaven Invade the Seven Mountains of Culture: 7M Chaplain Certification Guide*, and the quick read, *Become a Corporate Pastor*. Our coaching certification guide is *7M Coach Certification Guide*. Also see the shorter, *Become a Seven Mountains Coach*.)

This CV alone would not qualify me for the Melchizedek Priesthood, but Father called me into the study of The Priesthood some three years ago using only two resources: I listened to four or five of Ian Clayton sermons, and I read Nita Johnson's book, *Melchizedek The New Millennium Priesthood*. Since then the seven Spirits of God have taught me. This book is the next step in the ascent up the golden staircase to God along with the further developments through our Tipping Point Seven Mountains Gatherings. (See *Becoming Melchizedek Book II, Unto Fullness,* Chapter 4: The Coming Seven Moves of God in the 7 Mountains.)

Chapter 5: The Purpose of Melchizedek

Dominion

Make no mistake about it, we of The Order are about seeing that *"the kingdom of this world becomes the kingdom of our Lord and of His Yeshua."* (Revelation 11:15.) We are about bringing God's reign to earth and presenting Jesus with His inheritance as described in Psalm 2:8. *"Ask of me and I will give the nations as Your inheritance and the limits of the earth as Your possession."* If you thought that the Seven Mountains Mandate to take all of culture back created a stir as the left-wingers called us "Dominionists" planning a takeover, and labeled my friends Peter Wagner and Lance Wallnau right-wing conspirators, wait until The Priests arise. However, we are not going to take over the government. We won't have to as His government will be in our hearts and in our minds. (Hebrews 8:10, 10:16.) We will speak it forth, declare it, and His government will be established in our midst.

People do need to get right with God and get with His plan. I don't care what is said about the coming priests. We are making our plans known just like other groups are. We are in this battle to win it all for God. We *are* going to win this, and I tell you the enemy doesn't even stand a chance. We *are* to take dominion because God gave dominion to Adam and Eve, to man, in the garden. Stop backing away from joining in. Jesus is coming back—for His overcoming bride.

The church needs to arise and mobilize with a new fervency and a new boldness. She needs to stop backing down in the face of opposition. Believers must stop trying to merge into the world's groups and stop going in the wrong direction with sin. People say, "When the persecution gets bad, the church will arise." However, that is not historically when the church has arisen or when any persecuted people group has arisen. We must arise now before the enemy solidifies with persecution against us in one or many forms. If we wait until after persecution begins, then it will be too late. Look at Nazi Germany in World War II. In only five years, Germany went from a highly sophisticated and culturally diverse country to a nation that committed mass murders of Jews. This happened because Adolf Hitler arose to fill a vacuum. Thus, he was readily received by the people. Hitler was a man who misused rule for his own gain. Others have also actively abused power to fulfill their own ideologies. Abuse of power is a great sin in the eyes of the Lord.

How will The Order usher in the kingdom of God? Peaceably, like the way Melchizedek offered bread and wine to Abram. We will develop relationships with powerful and influential people like Melchizedek did as a king. We will operate businesses as modern-day Josephs. Or maybe we will run a city or advise statesmen, also like Melchizedek or Daniel. Joseph was anointed for business and anointed as an advisor. These functions of business and state will overlap some. The other side of our coin is that we will be warriors in the spirit, and the results of our warfare *will* manifest in the earth. We will

The Purpose of Melchizedek

speak and decree and work the works that He has called us to work while it is yet light. (John 9:4.) Whatever He says we will do. He will fully be our Lord, the Lord Sabaoth—the Captain of the Hosts.

The Order is moving us into an unprecedented level of the supernatural. If you want to operate in The Order, you must get rid of all fear of the supernatural, fear of the devil, and even apprehension of God. You may say, "The Word says the fear of God is the beginning of wisdom." That is correct. However, I am not talking about the healthy, holy, reverential fear of God, but am addressing an unhealthy fear of Him, fear of moving in His spirit and His gifts. Yes, around Him there are lightnings and thunders and voices! Glory to God, though! Bring it on, Lord. The world is going to have a full and complete revelation of who the Lord is, of what He is accomplishing, and of what the future holds for planet earth. They will see God's church come forth. All this is *to be revealed* through The Priesthood.

Order is coming by way of The Order under Yeshua. The opposite of the word order is disorder. I believe this Priesthood was established in heaven in ages past, but only came to earth in December 2012 with increase ongoing every year. Just like the Spirit of God brought order out of chaos in Genesis 1, Melchizedek has come to bring order out of current impending chaos. Genesis 1:2 KJV, *"And the earth was without form, and void; and darkness was upon the face of the deep. And the Spirit of God moved"* or brought order *from the chaos.*

December 2012 brought us the day that man's ancient earthly calendar, the Mesoamerican Long Count Calendar also known as the Mayan calendar, from the 5th century BC, stopped. The exact date was December 21st, 2012. The ancient seers and sorcerers could no longer see beyond this date. I believe from this point in 2012 we entered the Kingdom Age and the Melchizedek Era. This the revelation of Ian Clayton and I concur. We entered into the, *"For with God nothing shall be impossible"* age. (Luke 1:37 KJV.) God above ushered The Order onto the world stage on that day. Heaven's Priesthood Order came to earth that day to give God's people the spiritual structure and authority to operate in the Kingdom Age and to be the solution to increasing darkness.

The Order is the Final Order or dispensation on the earth. It will enable the third and final great awakening or reformation. Hear me, for this is The Order or framework that will put, as the Father has prophesied, *"all things under our feet!"* Hebrews 2:7-8 PHILIPS states, *"You have put all things in subjection under his feet'. Notice that the writer puts "all things" under the sovereignty of man: he left nothing outside his control. But we do not yet see "all things" under his control."* Think of that, not just under Yeshua's feet but under our feet as well. If God has selected you to be part of the first waves of this Order, and God is issuing this call to all, you will be one of the vessels used by Him to subdue all things under His Son's feet and your own feet! The first waves are going to pave the way for the rest of the Body. What an honor!

The Purpose of Melchizedek

Furthermore, this is The Order that is going to bring in God's original declaration from Genesis 3:15. The foot (or seed) of the woman will crush the head of the serpent (satan). Mankind has *never* been exalted to this level of power or authority like what we are going to experience in The Priesthood. We will know Jesus fully possessing us at strategic times to work His works through us. The mighty works, the greater works.

Then there is *"rule in the midst of our enemies."* Psalm 110:1-6 GW records what is coming forth.

> *The Lord said to my Lord, "Sit in the highest position in heaven until I put your enemies under your control." The Lord will extend your powerful scepter from Zion. Rule your enemies who surround you. Your people will volunteer when you call up your army. Your young people will come to you in holy splendor like dew in the early morning. The Lord has taken an oath and will not change his mind: "You are a priest forever, in the way Melchizedek was a priest" The Lord is at your right side. He will crush kings on the day of his anger. He will pass judgment on the nations and fill them with dead bodies. Throughout the earth he will crush their heads.*

The King James reads, *"make your enemies your footstool."* In this famous piece of Scripture from Psalms, David records YHWH talking to His Son about ruling and reigning. He foretells that His enemies will be brought low through His reign.

The young people will be many like the dew, and all people will be so moved by the majesty and the power of the King's reign that they will volunteer to serve the king and this will make all of His enemies bow low. The Lord has sworn that The Order of Melchizedek will "rule in the midst of God's enemies." Do you see how this Scripture is going to be fulfilled by us? The church has many adversaries and enemies right now. And they will only grow more numerous in the times ahead, but this does not matter. The Lord has selected us for this day to usher in the King's reign and the defeat of all of His enemies and our enemies. In our day, God is raising up end-time conquerors, Joel's Army, to be led by The Order! (See Joel 2.) It's the Priests who are going to wrap up the whole end-time eschatology. Yeshua's Millennium reign is coming.

Release of the Greater Works

Jesus said in John 14:12-14 PHILLIPS,

> *"I assure you that the man who believes in me will do the same things that I have done, yes, and he will do even greater things than these, for I am going away to the Father. Whatever you ask the Father in my name, I will do—that the Son may bring glory to the Father.* And if you ask me anything in my name, I will grant it."

The hour for the greater works to come forth is here, but they will only come forth through the greater priesthood. A greater than Moses is here and a greater than Elijah is here. A greater than Joseph is here. Because Yeshua is within us and with us in full.

Darkness is responding to the new authority in the earth that the Melchizedek Order wields. The Order has come to represent heaven's ways of doing things and to deal with the chaos that will soon arise in the earth. The Order will reign over the darkness and totally defeat it wherever the Priests are in operation.

Taking the Seven Mountains
Isaiah 2:2's words reveal God's highest mountain. *"In the last days the mountain of the Lord's temple will be established as the highest of the mountains; it will be exalted above the hills, and all nations will stream to it."*

In 1975, Bill Bright, the founder of Campus Crusade for Yeshua, and Loren Cunningham, founder of Youth With A Mission, had supper together at a conference and then met the following morning for breakfast. That night, God simultaneously gave these change agents the same dream, which they shared with each other over breakfast the following day. These men saw seven mountains that formed a larger, single mountain. God said that if they would claim the seven mountains, He would give them the large mountain that is the kingdom of God.

The message's meaning was that for believers in Yeshua to impact any nation they would have to affect the seven spheres or mountains of society—its pillars. These seven mountains of culture are business, government, media, arts and entertainment, education, the family, and religion. (Note that there are many subgroups within these main categories.) About a month later, the Lord showed apologist Francis Schaeffer the very same thing. In essence, God was telling these three change agents exactly where the battlefield is. Here in these "mountains" was where the culture war would be won or lost. And God assigned them to raise up change agents to scale these mountains and help a new generation of fellow Christian change agents understand the larger story.

The Order will assist those assigned to the seven mountains like WISE Ministries is already doing. The need is to develop mountain-specific strategies and deal with ongoing spiritual warfare and the expectation of fight. I believe my promotion to The Order is a continuation of what we at WISE have been doing for ten years in the business mountain and in all seven mountains—operating as apostolic/prophetic coaches and intercessors. We have been functioning in a Daniel 12:3 spirit of wisdom, kingdom consulting, seer realm help for our clients and their enterprises. We have been working to help businesses avoid potholes and wrong decisions. With this comes interceding for them and in the spirit, running ahead of the enemy's blockers who try to block God's communications and

The Purpose of Melchizedek

the blessings His messages bring. (See the *Intercession 2.0 DVD* series or my books on intercession from WISE Ministries.)

The Order brings an even a higher level of kingdom consulting and executive and spiritual coaching into a client's organization. Not to mention the higher levels of intercession under Melchizedek available to organizations that hire us. Power intercession and what it is now capable of accomplishing is exciting because this is going to allow mighty miracles to break in. Miracles will happen as if you were right there even though you actually are thousands of miles away. We are going to see that there really is no distance in prayer. Melchizedek consultants will employ the new spiritual technologies from the Lord of "ascending the golden staircase" and "going up into the heights." (See *Becoming Melchizedek Book I, Foundations*, Chapter 7: Functions of the Melchizedek Order and Chapter 11: Seeing into Eternity.)

Note: From Isaiah 14, the aims of satan are, "*Ascend to heaven and raise my throne above the stars of God. Sit on the mount of assembly in the remotest parts of the north. Make myself like the Most High.*" Satan has counterfeit heights: There are pagan stories of Baal and other gods assembling on Mount Zaphon. Zaphon means north. In truth, Mount Zion in the far north in Hebrew is Mount Zion Zaphron or Mount Zion the heights of Zaphon. And the heavenly Mount Zion, the real Mount Zaphon, is the real mount of assembly of God's heavenly Council which we of The Order *will* get to ascend.

Word of the Lord re: The Golden Staircase

*You shall ascend. You shall ascend the golden staircase for it is open to you, says the Lord, and some shall see it even in the meetings, and it shall be opened up—to ascend. For up to now, there has only been one stair step per year revealed, but I am now opening up the staircase for those that will be bold enough to begin to ascend upon it—but in an accelerated fashion. To my intercessors, run—run up the golden staircase, says the Lord! I stand at the top waiting for you, and my angels are already going up and down. Climb up and down with them; they will hold your hands as you traverse the stair (star?) case of revelation and provision for these times and return the provisions back to earth. I open up the access to the staircase right now, says the Lord. You shall sense a new level of angelic activity in your meetings. At times you will not be able to stand in my presence because of my manifested glory for what I am about to do—I am about to launch fire to the nations! (Song of Songs 2:14 KJV, "O my dove, that art in the clefts of the rock, **in the secret places of the stairs**, let me see thy countenance, let me hear thy voice; for sweet is thy voice, and thy countenance is comely.")*

Word of the Lord: Ascend the Heights

There are levels in heaven that I have not allowed my warriors to ascend to attain wisdom, revelation and power, but now says the Lord, the heights of heaven are open and new levels of power, glory, authority and administration to administrate heaven in the earth are being

The Purpose of Melchizedek

opened up. Ascend to obtain and to gather that which is needed and bring it to the earth. But, everyone must learn to ascend. Don't ask me to come down, I have already come down—you must come up in this season to obtain the resources, wisdom, and answers to perplexing problems. And they can only be found in the heights of the heavens, says the Lord. It is only for the lofty, those with lofty desires, lofty cries, those that want to abide in the heights with me. But not those with lofty ambitions, says the Lord—unless it's for my kingdom.

So, on the way are more seven mountains strategies, more solutions from the seer realm, more Josephs/Daniels arising as well as Melchizedek Priests. This is the purpose of our Tipping Point Seven Mountains' Unconferences that WISE does yearly. We bring together the modern-day Josephs and Daniels and now the Melchizedek's! We strategize together to build relationships for the seasons ahead, and we actually solve problems in the gatherings. Delegates (attendees) stay and eat together with us. Everyone learns together over two and a half days of highly optimized teaching sessions about all seven mountains. We honor your time by presenting information that you *need to know* for the upcoming year—sometimes lifesaving information. We give information that is key for the preservation of prosperity for you, your family, and your enterprise and employees. We ready you for future prosperity. Shameless plug I know, but it's truly for your benefit. (See TippingPointGathering.com for more information.)

The Order of Melchizedek will bring reformation to all of the mountains of society. There is not one mountain or sphere that will not be touched. Even targeted is the governmental mountain, which is currently so corrupt. (For more on the game plan to take the Seven Mountains, see Charles Robinson's series, *Let Heaven Invade the Seven Mountains of Culture*.)

Coming is Daniel 2:35 NASB and Isaiah 2:2 KJV:

> *Then the iron, the clay, the bronze, the silver and the gold were crushed all at the same time and became like chaff from the summer threshing floors; and the wind carried them away so that not a trace of them was found. But the stone that struck the statue became a great mountain and filled the whole earth.*
>
> *And it shall come to pass in the last days, that the mountain of the Lord's house shall be established in the top of the mountains, and shall be exalted above the hills; and all nations shall flow unto it.*

What about the stone that struck the statue in Daniel's vision? Remember Jesus' words from the New Testament, "*Did ye never read in the Scriptures, The stone which the builders rejected, the same is become the head of the corner: this is the Lord's doing, and it is marvellous in our eyes?*" (Matthew 21:42 KJV.) The stone in Daniel 2 was thrown at the feet of the statue, and the whole statue was smashed and blown away *like it never existed*. It's a parallel. The master builder ministry that Paul, the Apostle, began is coming back to the earth. God's government *is* coming down—upon His shoulders.

Meantime, He is building His church now, and, *"and all the powers of hell shall not prevail against it."* (Matthew 16:18 TLB.) The church's name is the *Ecclesia,* and this has to do with governmental reigning and ruling. The *Ecclesia* will become this ruling arm through the Priests of The Melchizedek Order, Yeshua's own order of government. Under The Order, Isaiah 9:7 will happen, *"Of the increase of his government and peace there shall be no end, upon the throne of David, and upon his kingdom, to order it, and to establish it with judgment and with justice from henceforth even for ever. The zeal of the Lord of hosts will perform this."*

The kingdoms of this world are becoming the Lord's kingdoms!

Evangelism and the Great Harvest of Souls

Melchizedek leaders will be at the forefront of the prophesied great harvest of souls. Revelation 7:9 says souls will accept Yeshua as Savior from *"every nation, tribe, people, and language."* Melchizedek anointing will be key in this. And the fact that Melchizedek dates back to Abrahamic times is key as well to reaching Jews and Muslims. (See the section, "Melchizedek Harvests," in *Becoming Melchizedek Book II, Unto Fullness,* Chapter 6: A Sacred Economy.)

Salvation of the Jews

From ancient times, the Jews have always looked for a king/priest. The Essenes at Qumran sought for a priest/king they called Melchizedek. In the Old Testament, Israel wanted Saul. The Order will satisfy Israel's longing for a king or a kingly priesthood. And then because we will point them to Yeshua, we will be instrumental in their finding salvation in Him. Thus as the higher priestly order in God, Melchizedek is key to seeing Jews saved.

The revelation of the Melchizedek Order has the potential to see the Jewish people come to Yeshua in great numbers. This is because Melchizedek predates Yeshua from an earthly perspective. The Jews seek after a sign Paul said. That is why so many of them are going to be deceived by the Antichrist because he will come in his own name and will deceive many with lying signs and wonders.

> *For since in the wisdom of God the world through its wisdom did not come to know God, God was well-pleased through the foolishness of the message preached to save those who believe. For indeed Jews ask for signs and Greeks search for wisdom; but we preach Yeshua crucified, to Jews a stumbling block and to Gentiles foolishness.* (1 Corinthians 1:21-23.)

As the Jews are used to a priesthood, how much better is our Priesthood than the shadow and Plan B priesthood of the Levitical system! Melchizedek is a higher order.

Reaching Muslims for Yeshua

Abraham is also recognized as the Father of Ishmael, the progenitor of the Islamic religion. The relationship of Melchizedek and Abram in Genesis 14 is a relational basis upon which Melchizedek Priests can evangelize the Muslim world. Because of Abraham's paternity of Ishmael, a bridge exists to Muslims to claim Yeshua, Melchizedek Priest and King, as their King and Savior. The Melchizedek Order with its history in Shem/Melchizedek can help the Muslims.

Prayer to Know the Savior Yeshua

If you want to accept Yeshua (Jesus) as your Savior right now, just pray after me:

[handwritten: REPENTANCE PRAYER]

"Heavenly Father, I believe that you sent Jesus to live a sinless life and to die on the cross for my sins. I acknowledge that I am a sinner and that I need your help. Please wash me clean. Jesus, your Word, says in Romans Chapter 10:9 PHILLIPS, *'If you openly admit by your own mouth that Jesus Christ is the Lord, and if you believe in your own heart that God raised him from the dead, you will be saved.'* Right now I believe that Jesus arose from the grave, and I do confess Him as my Lord and Savior. Right now I AM SAVED. AMEN."

Congratulations, my friend and new brother or sister in Yeshua. The Bible says that there your new name is written down in glory! Regarding your entrance into the heavenly city to come, Revelation 21:27 says, *"Nothing impure will ever enter it, nor will anyone who does what is shameful or deceitful, but only those whose names are written in the Lamb's book of life."* Send me an email if you said that prayer: charles@melchizedek.international, and I will tell you the next steps.

Once the nature and existence of the Melchizedek Priesthood are preached under the anointing, multitudes of the churched but unsaved Christians, Jews, and Muslims and let's *not* forget the New Agers will come into the kingdom of God. Many people are seeking for God. There is a God-shaped hole in each one of us that yearns to be filled and to have and enjoy relationship with the Divine Creator. To touch the eternal.

Chapter 6: School for Melchizedek's

Seven Years Under the Sevenfold Spirit

Word of the Lord re: Seven Year Training

It shall be a process, a Seven Year Process says the Lord, a process you have already begun. You will invite others into the process, into the School of the Sevenfold spirit of God. You are two years into the process. There are others who are further along in the process—already four years into it. I will connect you with them. The cycle has begun, the first seven-year cycle. Then there will be another seven and then another seven for a total of 21 years of three cycles of preparation. But it takes seven years of my training to become a Melchizedek priest.

I asked the Lord if the training could be done more quickly, and He said no. So, it is the case that other end of the age timelines are based around these preparation years for the Melchizedek Priesthood. Seven years is the most intense time of preparation for any calling in the kingdom.

All Melchizedek Priests will have identical core training, but will branch off into various callings as they fulfill the 21 years' experience. Each year will also entail a special level of training to deal with what is happening that year. So, let's think in terms of dispensations. In certain ways, the training of The Order as God's Fighting Arm will happen first. Then will follow the training of The Order as God's Kingdom Finance Arm. Finally, God's Priestly Administration Arm will happen last. The Kingdom Arm will set up the principles of God's Kingdom

Economy, and the Administrative Arm will set up ministry to the Father as He brings more functions from heaven to earth at the appropriate or appointed time. Thus, there will be different types of priests functioning depending on what year they begin and end their training and what is happening each year of the years that follow as far as operating in their specialty. (Note re: God's arm. When God talks about using His right arm, this means a supernatural saving. When God talks about using His left arm, this means a saving through natural means. Source: Nita Johnson.)

God has ordained your start date and your end date. Don't fear or be anxious and start thinking that you have missed your date or are starting too late. It's OK to start early. Only God can initiate you into the Melchizedek process. However, there exists an invitation awaiting you to Become Melchizedek.

Get ready as your training may be initiated through the reading of this book. I say *may* because only God can call you into The Order—The Order being a group of people set apart for the Lord's own priesthood. At best you are a part of it, and at worst you will understand more about who this order of God's creation is—now on the earth and destined to govern eventually the earth and all its affairs.

Understand that there are different levels within The Order and that there are different levels within heaven itself. For example, as Terry Bennett has said, "heaven has the realm of the least. These are those who just barely made it in." Compare this realm to the realm of those that live closest to the light of God and are just outside the throne room. And then there are those described in Revelation 14:4 TLB, "*For they are spiritually undefiled, pure as virgins, following the Lamb wherever he goes. They have been purchased from among the men on the earth as a consecrated offering to God and the Lamb. No falsehood can be charged against them; they are blameless.*"

I am writing about things that are all throughout the seven years of training under the Sevenfold Spirit of God—the Sevenfold Spirit assisting and directing me now. Nita Johnson calls them, "the multicolored torches of God." The Spirits appear in the colors of the rainbow. I have not experienced all of what I am writing about. Much of what I am writing is new. I have dedicated a week to write the core of the books, and God has been gracious in answering my questions. He is illuminating the treasures once hidden in darkness. From Isaiah 45:3, "*And I will give thee the treasures of darkness, and hidden riches of secret places, that thou mayest know that I, the Lord, which call thee by thy name, am the God of Israel.* Undoubtedly, I will revise this book as I learn and grow into my own expression of Yeshua in The Priesthood. What an honor for me to write this. Sometimes I feel like the least of the saints. God knows my heart. I am only worthy by His processes in my life. I have been obedient, and I have been teachable. However, He did have to purge me of my own self-life to an extent that is truly unchartered territory for the Body of Yeshua in order for me to write this book. I am well aware that there are several other books in print on The Order, but another step is needed in relaying the process ahead. My gifting from God is to tell you how actually to *become Melchizedek*—a how to do it manual just like the other *Become* books I have written such as *Become a Professional Level Intercessor* and *Become a Seven Mountains Coach*.

I hear the Lord saying, *"In due time. Get the instruction manual published first. Get my people on the seven-year Melchizedek journey."* I asked the Lord, "Am I the head?" And He answered, *"One of them."* There you have it. This book is my first replete with prophecy book. Kind of a daring work as it takes us into uncharted waters, but I am obedient. (On Columbus and uncharted waters, see *Becoming Melchizedek Book II, Unto Fullness*, Chapter 4: The Coming Seven Moves of God in the 7 Mountains.)

The Importance of the Baptism in Holy Spirit

For completeness, I must mention that being baptized into the Holy Spirit and coming into the fullness of life in the Spirit is essential. In fact, Holy Spirit gives the gifts of the Spirit as the fruit of receiving this baptism. See the Scriptural references to the spiritual gifts in 1 Corinthians 12 and other passages. And know that the Spirit baptism is the *gateway into the supernatural spiritual realm* in which a Melchizedek and especially the Professional Level Intercessor, PLI, operates. Without Holy Spirit, you will be unaware of spiritual forces, both good and evil, which are in operation in your life and in your sphere of influence. Without the Holy Spirit in fullness, it will be impossible to get to the root of the spiritual problems for which you are interceding. The baptism allows you to discern the true battle. The gifts equip you to exercise authority over evil and are very much your weapons of warfare. From 2 Corinthians 10:3-5 CJB, *"For although we do live in the world, we do not wage war in a worldly way; because the weapons we use to wage war are not worldly. On the contrary, they have God's power for demolishing strongholds. We demolish arguments and every arrogance that raises itself up against the knowledge of God; we take every thought captive and make it obey the Messiah."* Without being skilled in the use of these weapons of warfare, do not even contemplate entering this line of work. God will train you in spiritual warfare. Such training is a free gift from Him. As David said, *"You teach me how to fight my battles."* (Psalm 144:1 CEV.)

Scriptures Referring to Holy Spirit
Right now, if you need to, after reading the following Scriptures, just ask God to fill you with Holy Spirit. (And then see *Becoming Melchizedek Book II, Unto Fullness,* Chapter 2: Advanced Training.)

And be not drunk with wine, wherein is excess; but be filled with the Spirit (Ephesians 5:18 KJV.)

Peter: *"Fellow Jews, and all who are living in Jerusalem, listen carefully to what I say while I explain to you what has happened! These men are not drunk as you suppose—it is after all only nine o'clock in the morning of this great feast day. No, this is something which was predicted by the prophet Joel, 'And it shall come to pass in the last days, says God, that I will pour out my Spirit on all flesh; your sons and your daughters shall prophesy, your young men shall see visions, your old men shall dream dreams. And on my menservants and on my maidservants I will pour out my Spirit in those days and they shall prophesy . . . .'"* (From Acts 2:14-24 PHILLIPS.)

Repent and be baptized, every one of you, in the name of Jesus Christ for the forgiveness of your sins. And you will receive the gift of the Holy Spirit. The promise is for you and your children and for all who are far off—for all whom the Lord our God will call." (Acts 2:15-18, 38-39.)

I am going to send you what my Father has promised; but stay in the city until you have been clothed with power from on high. (Luke 24:49.)

But you will receive power when the Holy Spirit comes on you. (Acts 1:8.)

If you, then, though you are evil, know how to give good gifts to your children, how much more will your Father in heaven give good gifts to those who ask him. (Matthew 7:11.)

WISE Melchizedek University Online

We need to begin an online school for to train and unite The Order and begin to develop curriculum and practical exercises. Even now I am planning the launch of Seven Mountains University. As well, we will have Seven Year Melchizedek University, which will be an identical website portal.

What you have in hand is an instruction book, Foundations level, on how to become a Melchizedek Priest. But the outworking will take AT LEAST seven years for each of you. Welcome to your Melchizedek journey! You will certainly become activated and operable before seven years, but the *fullness* of your oneness with YHWH and your ministry in heaven and earth and your full maturity will not come before then. Again, there will be *many* life and spiritual exercises and lessons that God will take you, though, so don't worry about boredom with so much classroom material. Exercises are forthcoming in the supernatural, warfare, finances, humility, character growth, learning about God, angels, the enemy, fear of the Lord, wisdom, etc. All priests will be trained in the same areas but will find they have differing strengths and abilities as the Lord leads and grows them. Think of the term MBA, and change it to an MHA—a Master of HIS Administration! Each of us is on God's timetable. It may take you even longer than seven years to absorb all the material and training. Some will stop at year two or three or year six. But if you stop, know that God won't abandon you—He *will* be patient. Seven years, however, is the absolute minimum term—the quickest that one can attain to the Melchizedek Priesthood. To those who stop, you will not be considered a full Melchizedek Priest, but yet you will be more spiritually advanced than most prophets and apostles alive today. Can you see that this process is a Melchizedek evolution?

Note that The Order has the spirit of Wisdom. "*And they that be WISE shall shine as the brightness of the firmament.*" (Daniel 12:3 KJV.) Daniel is talking about The Order. Interestingly, our ministry is named WISE Ministries: Workplace, Inspiration, Support, Empowerment. God planned all along that we would help birth The Order by bringing strategic intelligence into the seven mountains and by pioneering the development of Spiritual Advisory Teams—SATs. (See our author/ministry bio at the beginning of Books I and II.)

Not only is there training by way of WISE, but also Melchizedek in heaven exists to train you on the earth like he trained Shem. You can do it! Just like Melchizedek above continues to train me through the seven Spirits, this Priest will train you. He will train you through this *Book I Foundations*, but not only through this book. After you have your core foundational training, customized lessons are coming. You will learn some things that I have not and will not learn and vice versa. But we will all be schooled in the essentials. Remember from the Old Testament: twelve tribes with various anointing's and destinies journeyed in the wilderness. God likes variety. "Why can't I just meet Melchizedek like you have and get his anointing so that I can already be like him?" you may ask. I asked the Lord the same question. His answer was and is: we need to be conformed into Yeshua's image by the transforming of our minds and through character development first. Otherwise, we would desecrate The Priesthood. Romans 12:2 KJV reads, *"And be not conformed to this world: but be ye transformed by the renewing of your mind, that ye may prove what is that good, and acceptable, and perfect, will of God."*

Remember, who you are becoming is the most important thing to God. There is a time for the laying on of hands for impartation, and impartation definitely comes in waves in the training for The Order. (See Romans 1:11.)

Issachar Coaches and Intercessors

The Issachar's
Sounds like a singing group, but oh that's *the Isaacs*, the family singing group out of Tennessee. . . . Just thought I would lighten things up as we start on our journey together. The Issachar tribe carried the Issachar anointing described in 1 Chronicles 12:32. This verse states (of the numbers of the men armed for battle),

"From Issachar, men who understood the times and knew what Israel should do—200 chiefs, with all their relatives under their command."

In this hour, God is again raising up anointed men and women who discern the times and know how to touch heaven to bring the wisdom from above down to earth on behalf of His greatly beloved people. His Issachar coaches and intercessors will advise re: all seven mountains or spheres of society. God is calling these anointed Issachar men and women to bring His presence, power, and revelation to leaders outside the four walls of the church—those who function in the marketplace. These Issachars will lead the charge to rally around the leaders who are changing all seven mountains or spheres.

The Issachar ministry will help empower, protect, and free such leaders from all kinds of bondages and hindrances. It will release the 7 Mountain operatives into their respective destinies. The sons of Issachar would go to war for the other tribes in a heartbeat. They arose early and awakened the other tribes with the sound of the shofar. The tribe members of Issachar—the name means "wages"—were the donkeys or burden bearers for their brothers.

The call on Issachar intercessors and coaches is to have an ability in praying for finances and giving financial counsel. We have seen tremendous financial breakthroughs for our clients from our advice and prayers, time and time again. Sometimes even before we start praying we see breakthrough. (See Isaiah 65:24.) One time a client's company doubled in size within twenty-four hours after signing a key contract! Can you see how your Melchizedek level counsel can work powerfully for clients or others?

Of Issachar, their patriarch Jacob said, *"Issachar is a strong ass couching down between two burdens: And he saw that rest was good, and the land that it was pleasant; and bowed his shoulder to bear, and became a servant unto tribute."* (Genesis 49:14 KJV.) This phrase again implies the act of burden bearing. We see that Issachar existed to help the other tribes. This son was to help the other "sheep." Issachar, after entering into Canaan, lived in the fertile Jezreel Valley and took responsibility for feeding all of the other tribes. Modern-day Melchizedek coaches and intercessors belong to the Issachar tribe.

Melchizedek will build upon the Issachar anointing that WISE Ministries has been operating in now for ten years.

Word of the Lord re: Melchizedek Reigning

Behold, says the Lord, I have put my words in your mouths. Speak what I give you—demonstrate the kingdom of God. Freely you have received, freely give. Show the world my great and terrible power. Show them my loving kindness and my grace. Be to them the shepherd that I would be to them Myself. Succeed in the areas that those that have gone before you have failed in. I give you my authority, I release it to you now. Wield it carefully but not sparingly. Carry my heart with you for I am truly with each of you. As I was with Moses, so shall I be with each of you. Be not afraid of their faces. (Jeremiah 1:8-10.) *Upon you has come* now all the law and the prophets, and there shall not be one jot or tittle that is not fulfilled. (Matthew 5:18.) Reign as my kings, like King David. Serve as my holy priests. I tell all of heaven, all of earth and all under the earth, "these are my beloved sons, today I have begotten you." I have birthed you myself for you are in a new age, the age of the kingdom and the age of the kings and priests of my Melchizedek Order. The days of enlightenment. The days of acceleration. The days of my starbursts, my kingdom Nova's. You shall shine like the stars of the firmament forever! (Daniel 12:3.)

(Please see my word for 2015 in Appendix A, "God is bursting onto the Scene in 2015," for more on Nova's and bursts and the bursting in of God.

Mobilizing God's Generals

Closely related to The Order itself is the training up and releasing of God's Generals into the Seven Mountains for invasion. The final book in the series, *Let Heaven Invade the Seven Mountains of Culture*, is the *7M Generals Certification Guide*. This guide details this process. Following is a summary of my purposes re: the Generals from MarketplaceGenerals.com:

> As God's CEO or business leader you need to be able to handle what the enemy can throw at you. For example, you are in Singapore, and it is 3 AM. You are fighting jet

lag, and the enemy is messing with you in spiritual warfare. You cannot get hold of the intercessors. What can you do? We will teach you how to handle these and other types of spiritual warfare situations, and not only that, but you will learn how to work with Holy Spirit and His angels and how to advance the kingdom of God no matter where you are in the world! No matter what situation you are faced with and no matter what the enemy can throw at you, God has an answer. As one of His Generals, you will lead the way, and you will ALWAYS be victorious.

That is not to say this victory will be easy. I have so far cast vision about the overcoming superiority of The Priesthood as compared to everything that has come before us. We can only write of what we have become. What you have in your hands is out of what I have become and what I am becoming. You may think, "Charles, you are not a big name." I respond to this with a "Yes, and I want to keep it that way." Jesus is the only *big name* that I want in my life. However, I do want this material to get out and with this of necessity my name will get out. Mine and Liz's life and our ministry are in God's hands. Promotion comes from Him.

The Order is "the overcoming excellence of God,"—the actual title told me by God. The war ahead will not be easy. There is the potential of great personal loss to us and even death in the journey and the battles that are coming. We are prepared to die for His cause. I guarantee you I am NOT going just to bow before these Islamic Jihadi monsters and allow them to cut my head off without going down fighting! My death will be a good death; an honorable death should the Lord choose this for me. My ultimate destiny is to minister before Him day and night in the New Jerusalem. That is where I am headed and what I keep before my eyes. And so should you. The New Jerusalem place that is so filled with the glory of God it is self-illuminating. The earth that we see is temporary. God has been preparing me all of my life for what is coming and the same with you.

I add for you: I am a warrior and a Five-star general of God. The twenty-four elders came to me and pronounced me a Five-star General four or five years ago. The elders, dressed in white with crowns on their heads, walked towards me as they gave this Five-star designation. And they told me the numbers of Four-star and Five-star generals operating today on earth. This level of a general in His army is equivalent to a Fleet Admiral in the Navy or a Field Marshall in the US Army. It is also equivalent to a Generalissimo or a Grand Marshall in China and other countries. Five-stars function only in a time of war. You are following someone who is not a novice. I have been through major battles with principalities. And I am not going to let some barbarians cause me to shrink back from His calling. I have already faced the Prince of Persia in battle and won. In battles in the spiritual realm against the spirit of Islam, we are going to see at least one billion souls come into God's kingdom under our Melchizedek evangelistic campaigns. Mine and those of others. These will be strategic spiritual military campaigns. Want to join me? (See *Becoming Melchizedek Book II, Unto Fullness*, Chapter 3: Apostles, Prophets, *and* Kings 2.0 for more on "Advanced Warfare." Also, a book to come from me is *Seven Mountain Melchizedek:, Melchizedek Strategies in the Seven Mountains*.)

Make no mistake about it, we are going to be targets of the enemy. Even now, as I complete the writing of Book I, it has been a time of great spiritual warfare. I warn: if the enemy can exploit any relationships or weaknesses in our flesh or *anything else* that he can use to hinder us in The Order, he *will* do so. We are in the fight of our lives and for the lives of those that God has given to us. But, today it's just like when the Apostle Paul was caught in the storm during his sailing voyage to Rome. God will give all those who travel with us to us as converts. We are to be their keepers albeit with the potential loss of earthly possessions and other stuff that we hold dearly. It's only stuff, it's only money, it's only a temporary loss; there is a booty that we have coming from the Lord above, and God and Melchizedek will supply our needs. (See Philippians 4:19.) And *do not forget*, we are to function as kings and marketplace people ourselves.

It's funny and ironic to note the mindset of Asian marketplace men and women. The Chinese businessmen I deal with are known for being such risk takers. Their attitude is, "I lost everything in the economic reforms, and then there was the introduction of free market principles beginning in 1978. If I lose everything again, I will make it up." I like this spirit. It's like China has the spirit of American enterprise from 200 years ago. Amazingly, I have actually sensed George Washington with me on this current overseas trip. If you question this, know that the great cloud of witnesses has an ongoing ministry to the saints on earth. (See Hebrews 12:1-3.) As well, they have a role in the Courts of heaven in deciding matters. The fingerprints of America are all over China. Our younger brother in terms of free enterprise is grown now and is greater than we are. So, we need to be careful in messing with China. Because I am called as a reformer to China and am from America, I know that there is more reformation that we can bring to the business/economic/finance, religion, and Arts and Entertainment Mountains in China from America. (See TippingPointChina.com re: the first WISE unconference in China.)

For more on the mobilization of generals in God's army, see *Becoming Melchizedek Book II, Unto Fullness*, the section "God's Dread Champions" in Chapter 8: The Melchizedek Revolution.

Chapter 7: Functions of The Melchizedek Order

Functioning in Fullness

What is the purpose of Melchizedek, Jesus' very own Order? The Order is called to co-create with God and co-administer His vast kingdom. We will rule and reign with the Son of God. The Priesthood is NOT divine, but in a sense Melchizedek is to function within the scope of the Godhead. Note the humility required of us in Daniel 4:17 AMP:

> *This sentence is by the decree of the angelic watchers And the decision is a command of the holy ones, So that the living may know [without any doubt] That the Most High [God] rules over the kingdom of mankind And He bestows it on whomever He desires And sets over it the humblest and lowliest of men.*

The Priesthood will perform the functions of many of the angels. God created Adam originally to perform this function. After man had fallen, angels were needed to perform many functions that man was supposed to perform. Now that The Order is coming forth, many angels will be reassigned. But first they must function as trainers of the sons of God as they enter into their fullness in Yeshua—the fullness that creation, itself, groans and travails to see.

These angels are assigned to us to train us in *their* functions, especially in advanced warfare, higher levels of worship, and other necessary functions for this hour. The seven Spirits of God will be training us in their functions, too. Isaiah 11:2 lists what will rest on us in the fullness of Yeshua: *"The Spirit of the LORD will rest on Him—the Spirit of wisdom and of understanding, the Spirit of counsel and of might, the Spirit of the knowledge and fear of the LORD."* Thus upon us: the Holy Spirit Himself, the Spirit of Wisdom, Spirit of Understanding, Spirit of Counsel, Spirit of Might, Spirit of Knowledge, and Spirit of the Fear of the Lord or holy reverence. Let's define these.

> **Holy Spirit:** Omnipotence, Omnipresence, and Omniscience. The attributes of divinity. However, we must further understand these Divine states in order to enter in and interact with the Godhead.
>
> **Wisdom:** More than just a word of wisdom—this spirit IS ALL WISDOM. From Daniel 12:3 AMP, *"Those who are [spiritually] wise will shine brightly like the brightness of the expanse of heaven . . . . "*
>
> **Understanding:** Divine understanding about the eternal plans and purposes of God. Understanding goes with omniscience.
>
> **Counsel:** He is "wonderful" combined with "counselor." Isaiah 9:6 TLB: *"These will be His royal titles: "Wonderful," "Counselor," "The Mighty God," "The Everlasting Father," "The Prince of Peace."*
>
> **Might:** Note Zechariah 4:6 TLB: *"'Not by might, nor by power, but by my Spirit, says the Lord Almighty—you will*

Functions of the Melchizedek Order

succeed because of my Spirit, though you are few and weak.'" Also note the dictionary definition from Dictionay.com: (Noun) 1. physical strength: He swung with all His might. 2. superior power or strength; force: the theory that might makes right. 3. power or ability to do or accomplish; capacity: the might of the ballot box. This spirit is God's capacity, superior power or strength, a part of His omnipotence.

Knowledge: More than just a word of knowledge. This attribute is God's Omniscience or a part thereof.

Fear of the Lord: Proverbs 1:7 KJV, *"The fear of the Lord is the beginning of knowledge: but fools despise wisdom and instruction."* This truth may be the most important of all for unless we get this right we cannot even be at the beginning of knowledge/wisdom. Without wisdom, we will not know how to operate in the other Spirits or divine attributes.

Once Melchizedek Priests enter into fullness, we will begin to direct the angels and not just work with them. We shall become greater than they though we started out lesser. From Psalm 8:4-6 KJV, *"What is man, that thou art mindful of him? And the son of man, that thou visitest him? For thou hast made him a little lower than the angels, and hast crowned him with glory and honour. Thou madest him to have dominion. . . ."* We have always been able to ask the Lord to dispatch angels on our behalf: *"Are they not all ministering*

109

spirits, sent forth to minister for them who shall be heirs of salvation?" (Hebrews 1:4 KJV.) 1 Corinthians 6:3 KJV says, "Know ye not that we shall judge angels?"

King and Priest and Five-fold Anointing's Combined

Melchizedek Priests as Leaders
The Priesthood will pave the way for other Body members to each walk in multiple anointing's. Remember, the priests carried the Ark of the Covenant on their shoulders with poles that ran through rings. We are God's delegated authority, His Melchizedek Priesthood, who will lead the church into its finest hour culminating in Jesus' coming back to receive His inheritance from the Father—"*I will give you all the nations of the world.*" (Psalm 2:8 TLB.)

God does nothing on the earth except through His empowered leaders and through His Spirit and His angels. Your very existence and calling into The Priesthood, assuming that you are so called, is a sign to the world and to the enemy that Yeshua's return is very near. Even at the door. We, as Melchizedek, are God's *divine enablement*. We are *the mechanism to get Him back to earth and take His true dominion*—His and our *full and rightful place*. (See 2 Samuel 15:25.) The fulfillment of Psalm 110:1-2 KJV is before us, "*The Lord said unto my Lord, Sit thou at my right hand, until I make thine enemies thy footstool. The Lord shall send the rod of thy strength out of Zion: rule thou in the midst of thine enemies.*"

Functions of the Melchizedek Order

The Order is the final puzzle piece God is putting into place. Indeed, it has been the missing piece ever since our High Priest came over 2000 years ago. We were not ready until now. He had to have a people that were mature enough to be able to handle the weight of this highest human and Godhead amalgamation and partnership in the universe. I feel unworthy before Him to write this. I feel like such a novice. I don't know Him at the levels I need to. My prayer, "Father, Jesus and Holy Spirit teach me your ways. I want to know You better. God, have mercy on us in help for what we are embarking upon."

The very powers of heaven are being shaken even now. Matthew 24:29 AMP is here in part, *"Immediately after the tribulation of those days the sun will be darkened, and the moon will not provide its light, and the stars will fall from the sky, and the powers of the heavens will be shaken."* As of this writing, we just completed the blood moon tetrad. This season is the time of this Scripture's fulfillment, and the earth is groaning and travailing for the manifestation of the sons of God. The Order is the full manifestation of the sons of God. Romans 8:19-23 ESV gives the picture:

> *For the creation waits with eager longing for the revealing of the sons of God. For the creation was subjected to futility, not willingly, but because of him who subjected it, in hope that the creation itself will be set free from its bondage to corruption and obtain the freedom of the glory of the children of God. For we*

> know that the whole creation has been groaning together in the pains of childbirth until now. And not only the creation, but we ourselves, who have the firstfruits of the Spirit, groan inwardly as we wait eagerly for adoption as sons. . . .

All hell is about to break lose, and its forces don't stand a chance. Terry Bennett remarks that the war ahead is not even remotely a fair fight. Let this get ingrained into your spirit. We have glorified satan for far too long. He is just a cherub and not the most powerful being in the spirit world—not by a longshot. Isaiah prophesied of satan reduced to nothing in 14:15-17 ESV:

> But you are brought down to Sheol, to the far reaches of the pit. Those who see you will stare at you and ponder over you: 'Is this the man who made the earth tremble, who shook kingdoms, who made the world like a desert and overthrew its cities, who did not let his prisoners go home?'

King and Priest

We are to be kingly priests or priestly kings. How about wealthy priests? We need to get familiar with this terminology.

With regards to Moses' earthly tabernacle The Order is through the veil and the apostolic and prophetic ministries are outside the veil. The apostolic and prophetic ministries deal with the earth and its people while The Order deals with that but also heaven, the cosmos and ministering to the lord

Functions of the Melchizedek Order

in the Holy of Holies. This is a major distinction. It's the difference between the ordinary priests which could only go in the inner and outer courts and the high priest who went into the Holy of Holies once a year. We of The Order will go into the "Holy of Holies", that is minister to Father directly and into the Throne Room often. Ezekiel 44:15-18 NIV says *"But the Levitical priests, who are descendants of Zadok and who guarded my sanctuary when the Israelites went astray from me, are to come near to minister before me; they are to stand before me to offer sacrifices of fat and blood, declares the Sovereign LORD. They alone are to enter my sanctuary; they alone are to come near my table to minister before me and serve me as guards. When they enter the gates of the inner court, they are to wear linen clothes; they must not wear any woolen garment while ministering at the gates of the inner court or inside the temple. They are to wear linen turbans on their heads and linen undergarments around their waists. They must not wear anything that makes them perspire."*

We are going to carry the kingly and the priestly. Note these verses:

Revelation 1:6 ESV, *"To Him who has made us a kingdom, priests to His God and Father, to him be glory and dominion forever and ever. Amen."*

Revelation 5:10 KVJ, *"And hast made us unto our God kings and priests: and we shall reign on the earth."*

Exodus 19:3-6 *"Then Moses went up to God, and the LORD called to him from the mountain and said, 'This is what you are to say to the descendants of Jacob and what you are to tell the people of Israel: 'You, yourselves, have seen what I did to Egypt, and how I carried you on* *eagles' wings and brought you to Myself. Now if you obey me fully and keep my covenant, then out of all nations you will be my treasured possession. Although the whole earth is Mine, you will be for me **a kingdom of priests** and a holy nation.' These are the words you are to speak to the Israelites."*

Functions of The Priesthood

Connecting to heavenly realms, encounters with God, going to heaven, etc. are great, but the Melchizedek priests are *always* before God's throne. Heaven is connected to them 24/7; they do not have to be shown a vision or be taken to heaven to have a truth communicated to them. God just communicates whatever needs to be communicated instantly to them. The Melchizedek Order is about efficiency in the spirit realm. This Order will operate at a higher level than even apostles and prophets and seers, many of which today have worldwide ministries. In essence, it's as if a new model Terminator is now out like in the science fiction Terminator series. So, devil watch out! These Terminators of the enemy's plans and purposes, if you will, are part of a higher spiritual technology. As I write this by revelation, I find myself asking the Lord, "Am I one of these new models and haven't even noticed it?" "Yes," I hear Him say, and I must accept it to be clothed in the new heavenly garments, the new mantle of The Order. He's asking, "Will you receive the new garments for yourself—for my purposes?" Why do you think

Functions of the Melchizedek Order

that the enemy has been fighting us so hard? We've had almost unending battles and lessons to be learned, humiliating situations to overcome, financial challenges to surmount—tests that have been in the waiting all along. The Sevenfold Spirit of God has been teaching us for years. We've seen the promotion of others and asked ourselves, "What is wrong with me?"
To be honest, sometimes I have felt inferior to others: their grandiose gifting's, influence in the world, and their God encounters. God has been softening my heart and pruning me as I've walked the Way of Melchizedek;

He's been developing my character for a much higher calling. Neville Johnson recently said that God cares more about who you have become than what you have done for Him. AMEN. Do know that the calling of The Order is absolutely the highest calling you can have on earth. It is also the highest form of sonship. (See *Becoming Melchizedek Book II, Unto Fullness*, Chapter 1: The Revelation of the Father.) God created the first Adam for this sonship. The Order is both the end and the beginning of our life in God. Remember, Hebrew thinking is circular. The beginning is the end, and the end is the beginning. To find out where you are going look back to how you began or started out. Want to see where a company founded on stealing someone else's ideas is going to end up? They will end up going out of business because their error happened at the beginning. Human life started in a garden not in a primordial pool. Human life will end up in a garden, a utopia. God's utopia.

And The Order is going to get us there. It's Yeshua in you that is *"the hope of glory."* From Colossians 1:27. Not glory from some gift operating which is external to you. In The Order, however, you operate from an inward Indwelling—you host the Spirit of Yeshua directly. The revelation is of Yeshua, Himself, within us. I am not talking about the Holy Spirit. At times, you will host the spirit of the omnipresent Jesus, Himself.

As Melchizedek people, at special times of service where Jesus or the Father needs us we will think Yeshua's thoughts, we will feel His feelings, we will act free of the natural mind, and thus do His work.

We will retreat and go away with Him for long times. (And such seclusion with the Lord is what separates the advanced Priests from those just learning. From the union that results, we will be used for hours a day and eventually, for some, even days at a time in a sort of suspended animation physically. Out of these special times, nothing shall be impossible for God or for God through us. (Luke 1:37.). Thinks of a hand and a glove. We are the hand and he will be the glove. Acting and moving and speaking through us, His beloved Order.

We will operate at higher levels of power and authority than Moses did or Elijah; we will see the greatest manifestations of the kingdom of God on earth that have ever been witnessed in history. And we will be the ones performing the acts! God

Functions of the Melchizedek Order

wants to take us back to the garden, back to Mount Sinai. Melchizedek is going to be operating through you and me even as God originally intended for Adam in the Garden. The Garden was supposed to eventually fill the earth and eventually the cosmos as Adam would be invited into heavenly administration of God's vast expanse. This original intent of God was thwarted by the serpent and his temptation but Melchizedek will get us back to God's original intent. God is asking us to move higher, and He *will* have a kingdom of Priests after The Order of Melchizedek. Literally we will say, "Mountain be removed and be cast into the seas," and it will obey us. We will be able to terraform—we will create islands from nothing!

We will engage spiritual forces, which we may not understand, but instantly we will have the mind of Yeshua and know what to do. Fear will not be in us; we will be fearless. We will not count the cost. Instead, we will be as the angels are. When God says, "I need you now," instantly we will be translated into another environment whether spiritual or terrestrial i.e. in the spirit or on the earth in a different country. We will live for the battle and for His glory and the glory of His Son, Jesus. We will receive supernatural strength and wisdom. Also our bodies will not need food or water for long periods of time.

Again, it's like we will be in a state of suspended animation.

We will instantly receive updates with strategic information about the situations into that we have been invited. The enemy will not be able to kill us. These levels are what God is releasing. Then, just like that, we will return instantly from other realms—we will be back in our bodies with our full faculties. We will fight, we will strategize, we will command, we will grow in new ways and function in new abilities beyond the simple spiritual gifts. We shall become Melchizedek.

Jesus said in Matthew 28:11 KJV, "*All power is given unto me in heaven and in earth.*" He did not say "on earth," He said "*in earth.*" We will minister heaven's authority and power in the earth! That means we will have power over the creative and destructive forces of the earth itself. Power against earthquakes, volcanos, lava, the fountains of the deep, even hell and the Nephilim.

. (For more on the Nephilim, see *Becoming Melchizedek Book II, Unto Fullness*, Chapter 9: The Battle Advances.)

Introduction to Melchizedek Intercession 2.0
Word of the Lord re: New Training for Intercessors

There is a need for new training and new impartation in the area of prophetic and apostolic intercession, and it shall be sent forth like arrows, even as rockets sent forth that shall pierce the stratosphere much like nuclear missiles do. Yes, my intercessors are going nuclear says the Lord. (Charles Robinson: "God is going to change the unclear and make it so clear that it is nuclear.") *The Spirit will so charge intercessory meetings that many will feel the surges and begin to operate in a new anointing of fire and evangelism, even the Elijah mantle, says the Lord. Many will be caught up in my whirlwind in this season and will spin like tops and the fire of God will be released on cities in this nation and the nations of the earth. Release them to release. Release the spinners, release the dancers, release the people with flags for a new anointing of release is coming, an anointing for warfare and an anointing to ascend the heights says the Lord.*

How does Melchizedek function in intercession? The Priests will change and advance intercession since Jesus, Himself, will be interceding through us as His Priests. And actually, that is the epitome of what a priest does—become the interface between God and man.

The reason that there is no "office" of intercessor mentioned in the Ephesians 4:11 list, *"He gave some to be apostles, some prophets, some evangelists, some pastors and teachers,"* is that intercession is a part of The Priesthood. It transcends the New Testament offices that Yeshua gave which are a part of Himself. The five-fold offices of Ephesians 4 are a part of Yeshua's administrative or Kingly function in the earth. The priestly part of Yeshua is seen in the intercessor. The Word in Hebrews 4:15 says of Yeshua, *"We have not a high priest that is not touched with the feelings of our infirmities."* Jesus is our High Priest, and He ever lives to makes intercession for us, the saints. (See Hebrews 7:25.)

In the Body, there are justice issues intercessors, prayer list intercessors, crisis intercessors, financial intercessors, governmental intercessors, intercessors who cover worship, personal intercessors, intercessors who plead for lost souls, warriors, and intercessors who cry out for nations especially Israel. Then, too, there are prophetic intercessors who access the very heart of God. Emerging is the field of Professional Level Intercession. (See the WISE 7M Certification training for PLI's.) Clients for PLI's include business, government, education, media, arts and entertainment enterprises, the world of religion, and the family. In short, the organizations of the seven mountains.

Intervention
Intercession 2.0 involves going from intercession to intervention. Intervention is basic to a PLI's job. As a PLI, you want your clients' spiritual destinies to be clear to them and to the world. Is the destiny of your client's enterprise being interfered with, distorted, or canceled out? Or is God's call on them getting through with clarity and consistency and reinforcement as needed?

The enemy will try to confuse or distort your client's message. He will try to interfere with the clarity of his or her message possibly through miscommunication or by mixture from some of the world's philosophies. Also, the enemy will take advantage of your client's own personal misperceptions re: what the Lord has given him for his marketing. Such can lead the businessperson to give out mixed messages about his product or service. As a PLI, you can help run interference vs. the enemy's interference, thus neutralizing demonic effects on your client and your client's enterprise. Read the experience of Daniel in Daniel 10:13 where second heaven forces tried to stop heavenly help from reaching him. Note: It's like in math where two overlapping sine waves cancel each other out.

Intervention means using interposition or the interference of one state in the affairs of another state. In science, interference refers to the moments when two or more light, sound, or electromagnetic waves of the same frequency combine to reinforce or cancel each other out. The amplitude that results is via the combining of waves. When you run interference, you stop being passive and become active in clearing the spiritual airwaves over your enterprise and the marketing of your products or services. Often the spiritual intelligence our clients need requires that we go from plain *reactive* intercession to *proactive* intervention by running interference. We do it the same way as football offensive fullbacks and tight ends run ahead of the halfback as he carries the ball. A fullback or tight end blocks prospective tacklers out of the way. Defensive players or PLI's run interference for the teammate who takes possession of the ball or the business going after marketplace penetration. PLI's go ahead of their clients in the Spirit and block the enemy so clients can move forward.

"The PLI runs interference on the enemy. He or she clears up the communication channels so clients can hear from the Almighty."

"Your client's enterprise is a tool of heaven to bring transformation to his region and sphere of influence, and it is specifically that destiny that satan will try to block."

In my books on intercession, I say, "Let's ensure maximum clarity between the Lord and His people. Let's send WISE informed, professional level intercessors and spiritual coaches into enterprises to teach leaders how to communicate their product and marketing messages well." (For much more on PLI intercession and also the use of strategic spiritual intelligence, see *Becoming Melchizedek Book II, Unto Fullness,* the section "Power Intercession" in Chapter 3: Apostles, Prophets, *and* Kings 2.0.)

The Eldership of the Earth

The Order is destined to be the "eldership of the earth" and ultimately the cosmos as well. Because of this, we need to start calling ourselves "Priests" — "Melchizedek Priests." That entails a lot as you know from reading this book. Confess from Psalm

Functions of the Melchizedek Order

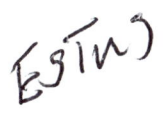

110:4, *"I am a Priest after The Order of Melchizedek."* Say it, and say it again.

Those of The Order, those Principal, Chief, etc. in the *office* of a Melchizedek Priest, not all of the Christian believers that are operating in some level of The Order, are the enforcers of God's will on the earth; they have His authority both on earth and in heaven. They are both kingly and priestly Christians that have been called by God specifically for this role, like the High Priest of old. Nothing will happen in the earth without their sanction and approval as they will always first seek approval from heaven. Already they are apostles and prophets. Therefore, Amos 3:8 KJV is valid: *"The lion hath roared, who will not fear? The Lord God hath spoken, who can but prophesy?"*

Ultimately, The Order will expose and eliminate the satanic and alien threat to the earth. This threat comes to us as the Nephilim agenda. (Note the book by Randy Demain: *The Nephilim Agenda: Exposing the Ultimate Last Days Deception*.) These beings, through deception, are basically trying to take over the earth and will urge the human race to submit to their evil wisdom and doctrines of demons.

They disguise themselves as benevolent beings, but they are at times very violent, fallen angels. (See more on the Nephilim in *Becoming Melchizedek Book II, Unto Fullness*, Chapter 9: The Battle Advances.)

- The elders are the enforcers of all covenants between

YHWH and man.
- The elders execute the judgment that is written.
- The elders hold court and administer justice in civil cases.
- The elders handle finances of the kingdom
- The elders are the government of God on the earth
- The elders consist of those Melchizedek Priests that have completed the full seven years of training and that commit to being active in interrelating with the other elders and assuming that role of responsibility

Always remember that Jesus, Himself, operated in The Order while on the earth. Jesus' operation as Melchizedek is the endorsement from heaven of The Melchizedek Order.

Introduction to Mystical Powers

What powers does Melchizedek possess? We have already seen from the Scriptures that Melchizedek has the power to put all things under Yeshua's feet and to administer the holy government of God. The Melchizedek Priests decree and declare things in the authority of God. Job 22:8 KJV states, *"Thou shalt also **decree** a thing, and it shall be established unto thee: and the light shall shine upon thy ways."* They well know the power of Words. (For how these advanced saints will literally move mountains, see *Becoming Melchizedek Book II, Unto Fullness,* the "Advanced

Powers" section under Chapter 3: Apostles, Prophets, *and* Kings 2.0.)

Secondly, these Priests will release God judgments through their mouths with their anointed words. (Again for more, see "Advanced Powers" in Chapter 3: Apostles, Prophets, *and* Kings 2.0 in *Book II Unto Fullness*.)

Working with Angels and Angel Armies
We, the inhabitants of earth, cannot hold back the Antichrist and bring in the kingdom by ourselves. By the way, it's not yet time for the Antichrist as the great harvest of souls must occur first and also the church must arise victoriously. We must have heaven's help, heaven's wisdom, heaven's backing, and heaven's resources to amalgamate with what we have down here. An amalgam *is* necessary—not the mercury by itself or the gold by itself but an amalgam. Together the forces of heaven and earth must walk out these times. We must now operate as a team. We must learn how to cooperate with and work with angels. We must know the Lord as *The Lord Sabaoth*—Lord of the Angel Armies. We must remember that our Commander-in-Chief, *the Captain of the Host*, resides in heaven. (See Joshua 5:14.) And it's key to take into account that though we do not see them, 2 Kings 6:16-18 KJV is true. *"And he answered, **Fear not: for they that be with us are more than they that be with them.** And Elisha prayed, and said, Lord, I pray thee, open his eyes, that he may see. And the Lord opened the eyes of the young man; and he saw: and, behold,*

125

the mountain was full of horses and chariots of fire round about Elisha." Thus, we must petition heaven for its will and the action of its forces to see the decree of Revelation 11:15 come to pass. From TLB, *"The kingdom of this world now belongs to our Lord, and to His Yeshua; and he shall reign forever and ever."*

As an aside, satan, as a cherub is not nearly as powerful as some of God's warrior angels. We have made him out to be bigger than he truly is. There are some angels that Lucifer would never mess with. In fact, while in Texas I saw the largest angel ever for me. He was at least one city block wide and hundreds of feet tall.

Chapter 8: The Church and Her Melchizedek Leaders

God is Going to Clean Up His Church

From heaven, the seraphim are coming to the earth to clean up the church. We see a foreshadowing of this work in Isaiah 6:5:

> *Then I said, "Woe is me, for I am ruined! Because I am a man of unclean lips, And I live among a people of unclean lips; For my eyes have seen the King, the LORD of hosts." Then one of the seraphim flew to me with a burning coal in his hand, which he had taken from the altar with tongs. He touched my mouth with it and said, "Behold, this has touched your lips; and your iniquity is taken away and your sin is forgiven."*

God is going to remove our iniquity, the root of sin or actually *why* we sin, and cleanse us from our sin. Isaiah's eyes had seen the king but his speaking or his lips needed to be purified. Isaiah's unclean words had been found out as well as the unclean words of the Israelite people. God is going to clear negative confession from the church—sinful words as well as words of unbelief. The Lord will act to remove the backbiting and the slander and the gossip within His church. And The Order, through our purity and the work that God has done in us, will be positioned to lead the way. The seraphim are going to cleanse us, too, I am sure. We will be an example for the others as we perform *"the greater works"* before the church. They *will* want to follow us and be like us. We will show them what is possible in overcoming this *"wicked and adulterous generation."* (Matthew 12:39 CJB.) Like Daniel of old, we will not bow down to the kings of this world system. Do read the book of Daniel.

Tithing
The initial act of tithing happened when Melchizedek, King of Salem and Priest of the Most High God, blessed Abram and also blessed God. In return, Abram blessed Melchizedek with a tenth of all of his spoils. In the days ahead, we will see the multitudes of believers tithing and even entering into Book of Acts level giving. In Acts 2:44 AMP, *"And all those who had believed [in Jesus as Savior] were together and had all things in common [considering their possessions to belong to the group as a whole]."*

Preparation of the Bride
Part of keeping the New Covenant and thus being a part of the Melchizedek family or priesthood will be the practice of Melchizedek Appointed Times, the Mo'edim. These are the Feasts unto Yahweh declared at the creation before sin and before there were Jews and Gentiles. Definitely, the Marriage of the Lamb and the Marriage Supper of the Lamb are a part of this feast-keeping. Among the definitions of *'mo'ed'* is *"rehearsal."* These yearly rehearsals are for our benefit. We must rehearse and re-hear His heart and His plans again and again. The Biblical feasts are rehearsals for the Marriage of the Lamb and His

Wedding Supper. (Source: Perry, Dr. David. 2013. *Back to the Melchizedek Future.* Raleigh: Lulu.)

Introduction to the Church of Philadelphia

It's foundational for Melchizedek Saints to study the Lord's words over the Philadelphia Church in Revelation 2:7-13. Philadelphia is us as victors and overcomers. From the PHILLIPS:

To the Church with opportunity

Then write this to the angel of the Church in Philadelphia: These are the words of the holy one and the true, 'He who has the key of David. He who opens and no one shuts, and shuts and no one opens.

I know what you have done. See, I have given you a door flung wide open, which no man can close! For you have some little power and have been faithful to my message and have not denied my name. See how I deal with those of Satan's synagogue, who claim to be Jews, yet are no Jews but liars! Watch how I make them come and bow down before your feet and acknowledge that I have loved you. Because you have obeyed my call to patient endurance, I will keep you safe from the hour of trial which is to come upon the whole world, to test all who live upon the earth. I am coming soon; hold fast to what you have—let no one deprive you of your crown. As for the victorious, I will make him a pillar in the Temple of my God, and he will never leave it. I will write upon him the name of my God, and the name of the city of my God, the new Jerusalem which comes down out of heaven from my God. And I will write upon him my own new name. Let the listener hear what the Spirit says to the Churches.

Note: the Lord's employing the Key of David is related to Philadelphia, the church that majored in brotherly love. (For more on this Key, see *Becoming Melchizedek Book II, Unto Fullness*, Chapter 3: Philadelphia Coming Forth.)

♪

The Forerunner Anointing

God always has His forerunners: men like Elijah, Moses, and John the Baptist. Their purpose is to go before and transcend one age and bring in the next age. David, especially, was a forerunner in the Holy Spirit. David transcended several ages at times. After he had sinned, Psalm 51 was his cry. Verses 10-11 AMP give us the picture of the salvation David experienced, *"Create in me a clean heart, O God, And renew a right and steadfast spirit within me. Do not cast me away from Your presence And do not take Your Holy Spirit from me."* David also in freedom ate the showbread allowed only for the Priests. (Source: Jones, Stephen E. (2011, April, 6). The Melchizedek Order—Part 2. Retrieved from http://gods-kingdom-ministries.net/daily-weblogs.) As a victor, he carried the head of Goliath right into the Holy

Place. So, too, is it with the modern Melchizedek. He has seen, participated in, and will bring others into the next age and even ages to come after that. Melchizedek, by his very nature transcends time. The High Priest transcended time when he went into the Holy of Holies and met with the Eternal God. When he applied the blood to the mercy seat, I believe that God in actuality went back in time to the point when there was no sin and that is how he "blotted out" the sins of both the High Priest and the people.

Melchizedek, King of Salem, was a forerunner of holiness, governing under God, and kingdom financial dealings. Jesus in John 8:56 AMP says, *"Your father Abraham [greatly] rejoiced to see my day (my incarnation). He saw it and was delighted."* How did he see it? Through meeting Melchizedek, The Principled One as I like to call him, as he operated in all of the kingdom principles before his time. The one who was the God-created prototype to *preserve the ways of God* after Adam, after Seth, after Enoch, and after the deluge or flood. Of only eight survivors of this cataclysm, Shem was chosen to carry the name and ways of God forward to the new world. Have you been chosen to carry the principles and the name of God forward for this generation? I know I have been chosen. I have a knowing and a sense of walking in a divine assignment from God. Why has he chosen me, seemingly one a *"least of the kingdom?"* I do not know other than that He knows I am utterly dependent on Him.

The devil always works through someone to preserve his line as well. This work of satan started with Cain and led up to Nimrod. Nimrod, the builder of the Tower of Babel was *"a mighty hunter before the Lord."* (Genesis 10:9 AMP.) Today we believe the Burning Man in the New Mexico dessert and the Nephilim/aliens are progenitors of satan's line. He is a father as well, don't you realize? He is not just the *"father of lies"* but according to Jesus those rejecting Him were the offspring of satan—literally. John 8:44 AMP states the Savior's verdict, *"You are of your father the devil, and it is your will to practice the desires [which are characteristic] of your father."* Alexander the Great, Napoleon, Stalin, Mussolini, Hitler—satan has his guys. The next will be the beast, false prophet, and the Antichrist. Do you see why God is raising us up? We are the world's last great hope. Hopelessly outnumbered, with radically less firepower in the natural realm, The Order will clean up this planet. We will be like Gandalf in *The Lord of the Rings*, but a more powerful and younger looking company, thank God! From *The Lord of the Rings*, the all-seeing eye of Sauron, the devil and counterfeit of the Sevenfold Holy Spirit, is actually not all-seeing, nor all-knowing, nor in all places at once. It will be very interesting when satan and his dark princes are cast to earth. There will be war in heaven before that happens and then war in the earth.

The Nathanael Generation

The people today and especially the youth are looking for real truth and for someone to lead them and to show them the kingdom of God. Psalm 110:3 GW says, *"Your people will volunteer when you call up your army. Your young people will come to you in holy splendor like dew in the early morning."* Or from the KJV, *"Thy people shall be willing (to follow You) in the day of thy power."* Arising in the earth is a mighty youth movement. I call these young followers, "the Nathanael Generation." I name them after Nathanael in the New Testament, a young man with a guileless heart who recognized Jesus as the Son of God, because they *will* see Him. (See John 1:47, 49.) Melchizedek Priests will lead many of them in the day of His power and in the coming day of *"the vengeance of our God."* (Isaiah 61:2 KJV.) The world and the world's youth will finally see the full demonstration of Yeshua's power in the earth and, too, the church will finally be the victorious bride that Jesus longs for in His coming back.

We will reign and rule with Yeshua for 1000 years. Melchizedek is destined to be among those of the Revelation 14 company of 144,000. From 14:3-5, the 144,000 are: *"those who had been redeemed from the earth. For they are spiritually undefiled, pure as virgins, following the Lamb wherever he goes. They have been purchased from among the men on the earth as a consecrated offering to God and the Lamb. No falsehood can be charged against them; they are blameless."* We will not leave the Holy City of our God i.e. the Melchizedek Order will stay continuously within the New Jerusalem. We will be those of Revelation 7:15 KJV: *"Therefore are they before the throne of God, and serve him day and night in his temple."* And Nathanael generation believers will participate. This younger generation will find how to walk with the Lord under an open heaven. (Do read my forthcoming book, *The Nathanael Generation: You Shall See Heaven Opened*. God commissioned me to write about the Nathanael's. And it just so happens that I named my only son, Nathanael.)

Note the following about Nathanael. (Source: Christianity.about.com.)

> Nathanael was one of the 12 original apostles of Yeshua. Little is written about him the Gospels and book of Acts. Most Bible scholars believe Nathanael and Bartholomew were the same persons. The name Bartholomew is a family designation, meaning "son of Tolmai." Nathanael means "gift of God." In the synoptic Gospels, the name Bartholomew always follows Philip in lists of the Twelve. In the Gospel of John, Bartholomew is not mentioned at all; Nathanael is listed instead, after Philip.
>
> John also describes Nathanael's call by Phillip. The two may have been friends, for Nathanael scoffs, "Nazareth! Can anything good come from there?" (John 1:46.) Seeing the two men approach, Jesus calls Nathanael a "true Israelite, in whom there is nothing false," then reveals that he saw Nathanael sitting under a fig tree before Philip called him. Nathanael responds to Jesus' vision by proclaiming Him the Son of God,

the King of Israel. (I note: Nathanael was the first to recognize Jesus' divinity, even before Peter.)

Church tradition says Nathanael carried a translation of Matthew's Gospel to northern India. Legend claims he was crucified upside down in Albania.

Backlash

Persecution

History tells us that typically the people who were of a former move of God persecute those of the emerging move of God. The Baptists persecuted the Pentecostals, the Pentecostals in turn persecuted the Charismatics, and then Charismatics persecuted the Apostolic/Prophetic church. So shall it be toward Melchizedek. Some apostles and prophets will not receive God's message through The Order to *"Come up here, and I will show you things to come."* (Revelation 4:1.) God is inviting now: "Abide with me; rule and reign with me." Ascending into His presence will begin to define the kingdom. Apostle and prophet distinctions are being rolled together into The Order. But the different functions will still be important and necessary on the earth. In my case, I operated first as prophet and then as an apostle. After that came my marketplace calling of kingship. I was a pastor for five years, a priest. Do you see how my multiple callings led me into The Priesthood? Can you see how your calling is leading you into The Priesthood? I hope so because I believe there are going to be at least 10,000 of us birthed.

Civil War in the Church?
As Melchizedek emerges, persecution of The Order will come. Be prepared, for some of the old wineskin will call you false and of the devil and every evil thing when they see their importance and their influence diminishing. Ever since 2012, heaven's focus has been on getting The Order in place. Of course, Heaven can multitask. To you, if you are one of the old church order, I say join us! If this is not God's will for you, then I'm asking you to pray for us. The subject of Melchizedek and the extreme seer realms that we operate in has the potential to start a civil war in the church, but I pray not. "Who do you think you are, calling yourself Melchizedek?" they will say. "You reign and rule with Yeshua in heavenly places?" "Really, God's High Priest?" I pray there will not be a backlash against this coming Kingdom Age Administration. However, rest assured, anyone calling this move of God "of the devil" will face a swift response from the Lord. You will have their lives in your hands. Remember, the Spirit of the Fear of the Lord and the Spirit of Might as it operated against Ananias and Saphira in Acts 5? We may just unleash such sudden death on our opposition, but, of course, only by God's directive. Actually, the Lord may do so through our words and we will not have a say at that time. Other times we will have a say. Actually, the

Lord may act without even you asking or you knowing. Sometimes we will be aware and other times not. Remember, we are going to host in us and through us the Godhead. Father and Jesus will have free reign to live, move and have their habitation in us. Such is the life of a Melchizedek king/priest. Thus, acts of God will often just happen spontaneously. We will have agreed to this type of Godly operation through us in advance.

We, His ministers, have been outside the veil in earthly ministries for too long. We must now go *through the veil* and enter into the Holy of Holies and minister personally as His high priest to Him. Think of this: You are called to minister directly to the Creator of the universe and enter into all that is seen and unseen! What a responsibility, what an honor, what a high calling. It is the highest calling that there is. Greater than Joseph, greater than Elijah, greater than Moses. You and I are standing on the shoulders of giants in the faith, but we will do the greater works.

Final Disobedience

Oh, yes, there shall be disobedience, even during the millennium. In fact, even Lucifer gets one more shot at humanity after a thousand years in chains, and he fights God for Jerusalem. He loses, of course, and gets thrown into the Lake of Fire where the Antichrist and the Beast and the False

Prophet are already under torment. So, may the church be warned and prepared for this final heated testing.

Lot Spirit

Let's revisit the story of Lot and the King of Sodom. First, Abram met Melchizedek in the Valley of the Kings after what is called the War of Nine Kings. The King of Sodom wanted his people back who had been taken by Abram and others in the battle. The King of Sodom was willing to enrich Abram financially. But Abram refused because he did not want it ever said or even speculated that the King of Sodom made him rich. (Genesis 14:23.) Abram had sworn to God that only God would make him rich and receive his testimony.

So Lot was taken away, and Abram was able to recover Lot after he had armed 318 servants to pursue Lot's captors. Sodom would eventually fall because of rampant homosexuality. Meanwhile, Abram had to deal with Lot now living in the midst of a perverse city. After he rescued Lot, Lot again returned to Sodom—a big mistake that cost Lot all of his possessions. Lot barely escaped with his life this second time as God, right after this, destroyed Sodom and Gomorrah with fire and brimstone. Believers must guard against the spirit of Lot—the spirit that would cause them to disobey and fall away in the end.

Chapter 9A: Priesthood Showdowns Coming

Priesthood showdowns are coming with the rise of Melchizedek to power. 1 Kings 18 describes in type a showdown between God's true Melchizedek priests, His Elijah's, and the false priests and prophets of Islam, the New Age, and other sects. Also, the showdown between Moses and the priests and sorcerers of Egypt in Exodus 7 is another great example of what is coming.

Do you trust God to protect your life during these showdowns? I ask myself this question, too. Yes! We boldly proclaim by faith, that when we are in the thick of things, God will come through for us. If I weren't personally supernaturally protected by certain major angels such as Michael as I travel the nations, I would not be here. God surprises the principalities, the big dark kingdom forces not just the little demons, as I cry out in weakness, "God, deliver me!" Because I am not a big name minister like some other traveling ministers, the enemy underestimates the firepower that I possess. I can underestimate it too! God keeps my warfare power hidden from them until His trap for them is tripped. God has taken me into the spirit realm where I actually see the principalities coming against me. He declares, "You can go no further against Charles." And God tells them, "look around," and the dark forces see that they are completely surrounded by the heavenly host!

Back to the coming confrontations. Many evangelistic campaigns will happen with multitudes saved in one day. And because of these much-publicized events, conflicts and confrontations will arise. God himself will force the confrontations. The enemy, though he knows he does not stand a chance, will be pulled into them. I love this! As Elijah challenged the 850 priests, the false prophets of Baal, and Asherah, and totally humiliated them so shall it be in our time. This time, the results are going to be staggering—much more so.

Babylon

The Word gives us a picture of the judgment coming upon the dark city of Babylon.

> **From Revelation 14:8**, *A second angel followed and said, "'Fallen! Fallen is Babylon the Great,' which made all the nations drink the maddening wine of her adulteries." Revelation 18:2 with a mighty voice he shouted: "'Fallen! Fallen is Babylon the Great!' She has become a dwelling for demons and a haunt for every impure spirit, a haunt for every unclean bird, a haunt for every unclean and detestable animal.* **From Revelation 17:2 PHILLIPS**: *Come, and I will show you the judgment passed upon the great harlot who is seated upon many waters. It is with her that the kings of the earth have debauched themselves and the inhabitants of the earth have become drunk on the wine of her filthiness.*

Just what is Babylon in the Bible? My thought is that Babylon is satan's city, like the pagan Babylon of the Old Testament. It's his building, like the city that Nimrod built with the Tower of Babel. Satan loved Nimrod as he was the source of the purest form of evil of that day and truly satan's son as he exhibited satanic DNA with his penchant for reaching for power and for the stars. Isaiah 14:13-14 KJV records Lucifer's boast, "*I will ascend into heaven, I will exalt my throne above the stars of God: I will sit also upon the mount of the congregation, in the sides of the north: I will ascend above the heights of the clouds; I will be like the most High.*"

I believe Babylon exists in part all over the world. It is more an evil spiritual domain than an actual zip code at this time. In a way, it is kind of like the New Jerusalem we access now though in a material way not here yet. (See Galatians 4:6 on the Jerusalem above.) Worldly business, wherever it is conducted, can be thought of as Babylon. Revelation 18 tells of Babylon, "*By your merchandise are all the cities of the world defiled.*" Whether Babylon coalesces into an actual powerful, earthly city remains to be seen. Satan's kingdom is everywhere on the earth where evil men and their sin abounds. Greed, lust, avarice, injustice, the false, abuse, etc. are all a part of Babylon and her commerce.

Two Cities

Ultimately, the book of Revelation portrays two cities: "Mystery Babylon" and "New Jerusalem." No longer are they the original earthly cities, but they are spiritual cities. The main theme of history is the conflict between these cities, with each claiming dominion over the earth. In every age, men side with either one city or the other. From the Biblical perspective, first Jerusalem and then the New Jerusalem are the genuine inheritors of the kingdom, while Babylon and then Mystery Babylon are revealed as the usurpers or counterfeits. (Source: Jones, Stephen E. The Melchizedek Order—Part 1. (2011, April, 5). Retrieved from gods-kingdom-ministries.net/daily-weblogs/2011/04-2011/.)

The Melchizedek Order as it emerges will stand against the false king/priests of Babylon. These false king/priests will also be very authoritative and powerful and deceptive—experts in the dark or black arts. But we will win.

False Melchizedek's

"Belchizedek"

No, this is not Belichick, as in Bill Belichick the head coach of the New England Patriots football team in America. I am talking about the Jezebel Principality masquerading as the true Melchizedek. For this Jezebel spirit, I use the term "Belchizedek" combining "bel," a variant of the word "Baal" with "Melchizedek." Seriously, folks, we know that the enemy counterfeits what God does so we must expect these very good looking imposters to show up. We must pray for discernment of spirits. (1 Corinthians 12:10.)

False Priesthoods

The Catholic Church

Not only are false Melchizedek's arising but also false priesthoods. The Catholic Church's false papal priesthood stands in conflict with the Melchizedek priesthood. How important is the true priesthood of God called to fully represent Him? After the golden calf incident of Exodus 32, we must remember that YHWH could have wiped all the Israelites out under His blood covenant right and started over. And He would have had not Moses pleaded with Him on their behalf.

The Mormon Enterprise

Mormonism, too, is a false priesthood. Revelation 22:18 clearly states God's warning: *"I warn everyone who hears the words of the prophecy of this scroll: If anyone adds anything to them, God will add to that person the plagues described in this scroll."* The Apostle Paul goes on to say in Galatians 1:8, *"But even if we or an angel from heaven should preach a gospel other than the one we preached to you, let them be under God's curse!"*

Mormonism started when the angel of Moroni appeared unto Joseph Smith and gave him the revelation of Mormonism. This Mormon book was adding unto the Word of God. If you *are* involved in Mormonism, my dear reader, do get out. The Order of Melchizedek that Mormons teach is not the True Order because this false order detracts from Jesus! The Book of Mormon adds unto The Holy Bible.

Why do we need it? Everything and more that Mormonism offers you, we are being offered in The Order. And it is done through God's progressive restoration and in the fullness of time – according to God's timetable. We are right on time!

Islamic Clerics

Islam does not have priests per se, but they do have clergy such as Mullah's, Imam's, Sheiks, and Ulama's. My understanding is that the Imam's can do whatever they want. There is very little if any moral standard over them. Many books have been written warning against Islam. I say, if you are involved in this political system, get out!

There will be wars between the priesthoods—God's true priests against the false priests of the Catholicism of the Pope and his supporting bishops, The Imams and other leaders of Islam, the false Melchizedek's of the New Age and the cults, the high priests of witchcraft, and satan's counterfeit prophets and priests.

Other False Priests and Their Organizations

In a casual survey of the web, the amount of false information and spiritual mumbo-jumbo and deception is massive. The false teachers are claiming to give the Melchizedek inductee immortality and great powers. The enemy is working to cause so much confusion by way of the false that it is very hard to discern the true. Fallen angels are masquerading as Melchizedek. This arena is a true battlefield filled with landmines. What do we do about this flood of the deceptive? When the true comes all deceivers will be exposed.

Nephilim Societies/Aliens and UFO's

The Nephilim are coming again on the earth. And God will enlist Melchizedek priest/warriors against them. Do read *The Nephilim Agenda: Exposing the Ultimate Last Days Deception* and *The Nephilim Resurgence* by Randy DeMain.

The elite Melchizedek forces *will* have the spiritual firepower to effect both the natural and spiritual realms. We will confront our enemies with the spiritual weaponry that can take them out. There is much to learn about these areas of warfare, and I am right now asking the Lord for His tools and weapons and training by the angels in how to use them. Often God's strategy or weaponry actually IS the deployment of angels. They will accompany us, but we need as well to be skillful and useful to the kingdom and know how to wield spiritual weapons ourselves.

9B: The War Ahead

The spiritual and cultural atmosphere will not change everywhere on the earth but only where God is allowed freedom to operate, minister, and move. Darkness is going to increase in the areas where God is not "allowed" to change things. Thus the duality of Isaiah 60. Verses 1-3 AMP reveal:

> *Arise [from spiritual depression to a new life], shine [be radiant with the glory and brilliance of the Lord]; for your light has come, And the glory and brilliance of the Lord has risen upon you. "For in fact, darkness will cover the earth And deep darkness will cover the peoples; But the Lord will rise upon you [Jerusalem] And His glory and brilliance will be seen on you. "Nations will come to your light, And kings to the brightness of your rising.*

The Order vs. the Forces of Hell

Lucifer is jealous and envious because coming under Melchizedek is a level of power, authority, and connectedness of heaven and earth never before seen. There will be no more room in the second heaven for satan when earth and heaven meet and join forces in fullness. Because of this force, Lucifer and his fallen ones will have no choice during the early stage of the Great Tribulation but to be thrust to earth and eventually cast into the lake of fire. In the case of Lucifer, he will soon be bound in chains for 1,000 years.

The UN

God is restoring The Order because this company will be the enforcing arm of His kingdom. The Order will establish order.

But this will not be like what the United Nations is planning with its 17-tenet Agenda 2030 Global Sustainability Plan, a plan to enslave all the people on the globe to the big corporations such as Monsanto, DuPont, BASF, etc. The UN desires a fascist order over the earth. Satan's plan is the United Nations Agenda 2030. God's plan is The Order of Melchizedek. Have I made myself clear? (See the Appendix in *Becoming Melchizedek Book II, Unto Fullness*, on the United Nations Agenda 2030 for a list of the 17 tenets.)

The New World Order and the Globalists

Our world today is run from behind the scenes by globalist groups that call themselves the Illuminati. They have other names such as the Council of 300, the Elite, etc. The members are the wealthy families of the past such as the Rothschild family, the J. P. Morgan clan, the Rockefellers, and some of the new wealthy such as the Bill Gates family. Their views on the UN Agenda 21, the UN Sustainability 2030 Plan, and more are public—published.

The globalists have used the crusade to "heal" global warming (which at the time of the final editing of this book, a plan to address this was just passed in France) and fix excess carbon emissions to transfer wealth from the rich, developed nations to themselves under the guise of helping the poor. If this sounds harsh, it is but it is also a reality. Their plans are to place the world's population in debt to them. The globalists also want to consign most of the earth's populations to cities so that they can be more easily "managed" and to give the illusion of overpopulation. The USA, in truth is the only thing that stands in the way and specifically, our sovereignty granted by our constitution. When you hear of global treaties and Trans-Pacific Partnerships and global courts, these are the words and projects of the Elite and those that try to eliminate any nations' sovereignty. Treaties trump the USA's constitution once ratified. The truth is satellite data confirms that we have had no significant global warming of the earth for the past 18 years. The global warming agenda is a ruse for gain and has been elevated to the level of a global religion.

See the book *Dark Winter: How the Sun Is Causing a 30-Year Cold Spell"* by John Casey. Casey says that the sun has entered into a 30 year "solar minimum" era that will dramatically affect agriculture.

Antichrist, Beast, and False Prophet

As God's people, we have our seven mountains that will one day be under the one great mountain, Mount Zion. We work to take the seven mountains of society for Yeshua's kingdom. And the world order has its hills, such Aventine Hill, Palatine, Hill, etc.— the Seven Hills of Rome. War is ongoing between one kingdom, the kingdom of Light, and the other, the kingdom of darkness.

From Colossians 1:13-14, *"He rescued us from the power of darkness, and re-established us in the kingdom of His beloved Son, that is, in the kingdom of light."* (For a more detailed report on the war between the two kingdoms see *Becoming Melchizedek Book II, Unto Fullness,* Chapter 9: The Battle Advances.)

Last Days' Anointing Against the Lawless Ones

Word of the Lord re: Anointing and Protection Against the Lawless

I have called each of you as enforcers of my righteousness to judge those that are the lawless ones. My Word says as it was in the days of Noah so shall it be in the coming of the Son of Man. Many, even of my people are sleeping when the ship is going down. Many of my people are being seduced into a slumber—the sleep that asks as of old, "where are the signs of His coming and of the end of the age?" The age has already ended on your watch, and a new kingdom age has begun. Wake up! Join my army, join what I am doing in the earth. Do not become a part of the problem, but be a part of the solution. Many of my people are going to fight in the wrong way, fight in their flesh, and many shall take up and use arms and many shall perish. My plan is to fight, yes, but fight under my ordained generals, my Melchizedek Order. Then you shall be in proper alignment and be protected by me, says the Lord. Do not allow the spirit of lawlessness and hatred and murder to enter your hearts. For this, you shall surely perish. Take everything into prayer. Cry out to me for the answers for your specific situations. If you operate as the world does then you shall perish with the world. Yes, defend yourselves, and you will need to. Yes, prepare with food and water and save some for others as well. Do what you can do, and leave the rest to me. I will show you what to do. I will visit you, my people. I will spare you, and I will save you.

God is anointing for battle and anointing Saints to overcome. (For more see *Becoming Melchizedek Book II, Unto Fullness,* Chapter 9: The Battle Advances.)

Chapter 10: The Coming Kingdom Economy

World Financial Meltdown

I see the financial systems of the world such as the Federal Reserve, the Bank of International Settlements (BIS), the International Monetary Fund (IMF), the World Bank, Society for Worldwide Interbank Financial Telecommunications or S.W.I.F.T. money transfer system, Shanghai Gold Exchange, the new Oil Bourse trading platform with Russia and China, all as large glaciers. Glaciers are mostly underwater—just like our financial system. They are slow-moving and also usually melt very slowly—like in global warming? Also, sometimes glaciers increase in size in periods of cooling. Think: the Chinese Yuan being added to Special Drawing Rights (SDR) currency and thus increasing the Chinese voting share while eliminating USA veto power.

However, I see the Lord breathing His hot breath in the spirit upon these global glacial financial systems. They are now melting much more rapidly. The more the experts employ various methods to try and prop up the financial systems—Quantitative Easing, the Asian Contagion with devaluation of the Yuan, a Greek exit from the EU with ongoing bailout talks—the quicker the glaciers are melting. The glacier picture is a visual of what is happening now in 2015. The financial meltdown of the old debt-based economy, of which the USA/Europe has had hegemony via the IMF and Federal Reserve for the last one hundred years plus, will result in two totally new systems. In the end: an Asian/Russian-led consortium and a kingdom of God-led consortium. For God's people there will be the kingdom system or perhaps multiple loosely coupled systems. Only those people locked into the new system of the world will run into buying and selling problems. God's people operating in God's Kingdom Economy will fare differently. However, all will feel the shakings as the old system totally melts down before our eyes. 2015 is the beginning, but the meltdown will continue into 2016 and beyond.

The Transfer of Wealth

Proverbs 13:22 AMP reveals that *"And the wealth of the sinner is stored up for [the hands of] the righteous."* Coming is a transfer of wealth from the old systems to the new systems. Remember, this is not a destruction of wealth but a change in the ownership of wealth. Psalm 24:1 AMP states, *"The earth is the Lord's, and the fullness of it, The world, and those who dwell in it."* The world's wealth is God's. It has been laid up for you and me, but we must listen to His prophets, listen to His Joseph's, and listen to His Melchizedek Priests on how to unlock *"the treasures of darkness, and hidden riches of secret places"* —the treasures are inside the glacial ice. (Isaiah 45:3 KJV.)

God is bestowing a modern-day Cyrus anointing and bringing forth modern-day Cyrus players. These Cyrus's will be like the Old Testament Cyrus, who brought release from captivity to God's people after seventy years. Isaiah 45:1-2 NIRV describes this anointing level, *"Cyrus is my anointed king. I take hold of his right hand. I give him the power to bring nations under his control. I help him strip kings of their power. . . "*

I also see that in the core of the financial glaciers are not just the gold, silver, and precious stones but also the industries that led to these vast fortunes such as oil, kerosene, railways, steel, plastics, etc. (See The History Channel's *The Men Who Built America.*) God is going to unlock and launch such a new wave of innovation that entirely new industries such as robotics, nanotech, cures for every major disease, etc. will result in vast new fortunes and redistribution of wealth. What communism and socialism promised—economic redistribution—God will bring about in His way in this hour. And He will do it through innovation through you and me!

Frozen Assets

Inside of many of these glacier-like financial systems is wealth that has been hidden for decades, hundreds of years and even generations. It is the "old money" of the wealthiest families and dynasties of the world. I see the wealth of the nations and the wealth of the wicked being unlocked. Not only that, but many of the monies held in abeyance for God's people are being unlocked as well. What has been frozen assets are now becoming thawed out assets and transferred around the world as when a

The Coming Kingdom Economy

glacier melts and water enters the waterways of the world through the ocean's currents.

The transfer involves the money and other financial instruments and assets such as gold and silver moving into newer financial structures like the BRICS New Development Bank—Brazil, Russia, India, China, and South Africa. The Federal Reserve is merging with the PBOC—The Peoples' Bank of China. This global money system is run by the "Money Masters" or bankers with the goal of world economic domination. Ultimately it will comprise the "Beast" system outlined in the Bible with its mark. Know that the mark of Revelation 13:16-17 KJV is coming: *"And he causeth all, both small and great, rich and poor, free and bond, to receive a mark in their right hand, or in their foreheads: And that no man might buy or sell, save he that had the mark, or the name of the beast, or the number of his name."*

Transfer of Territory

Territory will be turned over to believers as well. For example, I have come to China to bring the kingdom of God to this land and to transfer territory for my King. I just do what I do, and the territory of the enemy begins to fall into the hands of Christians—a transfer over to God's kingdom. We need not worry about the end-time wealth transfer so much. We need to focus on *the end-time territory transfer* for when we do this *both* the land and the money will come to us. Now, that's good preaching! I give businessmen English lessons that just happen to be spiritual lessons related to the kingdom. You can use your work in a similar way.

Gold Standard Stability

He Who Owns the Gold Make the Rules

A gold-backed system must be in place to bring stability. Russia has already entertained this idea as well as has China. By the way, China now holds vast amounts of gold, probably the most in the world of any country. However, off-balance sheets may reveal trillions in gold owned by certain wealthy families—enough to pay off the national debts of every country in the world. Remember the wealth is *inside* the icebergs—entrenched in the ice. And *entrenched* means: *of an attitude, habit, or belief, firmly established and difficult or unlikely to change; ingrained*. (Source: https://www.google.com/#q=entrenched+definition.) J.P. Morgan has accumulated an estimated 50 million ounces of silver. What do they know that we should know? What I am telling you!

The new Kingdom Financial System will be gold backed. It has to be. Fiat currency is what got us into this problem in the first place. For example, in 1971, President Nixon took the USA off the gold standard. As a result, the Federal Reserve could export dollars and American inflation overseas via the Eurodollar and the Petrodollar without having to back those dollars in gold—

the US dollar being the world's reserve currency. Thus, we adopted fiat currency. Once off the gold standard, the US began to accumulate unsustainable amounts of debt and run yearly deficits. Today, our national debt stands at 18 trillion dollars.

And the interest on this in ten years will consume up to a full half of our gross domestic product (GDP).

(For more on the Kingdom Economy of God see *Becoming Melchizedek Book II, Unto Fullness*, Chapter 6: A Sacred Economy.)

Chapter 11: Seeing Into Eternity

Come Up Here: Revelation 4 Encounters

Word of the Lord re: Come Up Here

The Lord says that I am activating my Priests at this time. I am calling you higher says the Lord, upwards, and into me. There is no space and time where I am taking you. Time will cease, and you will enter me, my realms, my heart, my mind, for I am giving you my mind—not just the mind of Yeshua but the mind of the Godhead and how we function. I am inviting you now into the Godhead. The same Trinity that Isaiah was invited into when he wrote, "Come now let us reason together," says the Lord, "though your sins be as scarlet they shall be as snow, though they be red like crimson, they shall be as wool." We are calling you up to reason with Us—to strategize with Us and with the twenty-four elders and with the cherubim and the seraphim. With this call is a new level of authority and a new assignment for you. How about the great cloud of witnesses? They are not only cheering you on; they have been assigned to pray for you and to help you complete your assignments. The veil between heaven and earth is being torn. There is free access between heaven and earth where the portals are opened and in the cities and territories where my Order is operating. You get to do new things in me, exciting things. You are going on a journey with me. This book is an instruction manual in how to operate in The Priesthood, how to function in The Priesthood, and how to administrate my ordinances and my laws.

The Brink of Eternity

Today, we are standing at the brink of eternity looking towards a better day. Jesus said in John 8:56, *"Abraham desired to see my day, and he saw it and rejoiced."* I, too, desire to see another day — the Day of Melchizedek. Do you desire to see that day and live in that day? It is here! This day of Melchizedek I have been created to see and help birth! I tell you I can see the day of the fullness of The Order. I am at the threshold right now in the spirit, and I can see this day shining forth. It looks like the cosmos and is bright and colorful with the vast expanse of it. I am leaning over and seeing the luminaries or the Priests of The Order as they shine throughout the cosmos. Each looks like a star and has his or her own galaxy. Note Daniel 12:3 AMP, *"Those who are [spiritually] wise will shine brightly like the brightness of the expanse of heaven, and those who lead many to righteousness, [will shine] like the stars forever and ever."* I can see into eternity and see all of you Melchizedek's. God has a place for you and me in His universe to create, maintain, and manage it — His galaxies!

Melchizedek Transcends Time

God, Himself, transcends time through The Priesthood. And you as a Priest will ultimately not be limited by time. Again, Melchizedek had no beginning and no ending as declared in Scripture. This means that he was not bound by time. If it was true for him it is true for us.

The Priesthood Of course, we will need heaven's assistance for time travel. Mainly we will operate concerning things in the future. Just like God, we will, *"call those things which be not as though they were."* (Romans 4:17 KJV.) Our job, as Melchizedek 2.0 or next generation Melchizedek, is just as it was with Melchizedek 1.0. We are to bring the Divine Order from heaven to Earth. Note that everything God does, satan perverts and twists. So, there are many things to rectify on this earth using God's spiritual principles. Remember, we are heaven's priests with an authority both in heaven and in the earth.

[Matt 18:18]

We are to bring back to earth in our time what we see as seers. When we see it, we shall possess it. We will tap this creative force of the universe. Time is actually energy. E=MC2 says energy is mass times the speed of light squared. We shall bring the Light of God, His revelation, back into our time and walk in it. I see heaven's revelation as building materials for a road or a path that we will pave into the future. God told me that the Book of Revelation, the Book of Daniel, and the Book of Zachariah, all say what is going to happen in the end-time, but it's the Melchizedek Priests who will pave the way as to how and when the events such as the seals (which have already begun), the trumpets, the woes, and the bowls/vials of Revelation will actually happen. I do not want to argue Preterism of Partial-Preterism, *Victorious Eschatology*, the book by Harold Eberle, the Book *Raptureless* by Jonathan Welton, as these theological views are not pertinent to this material as even if we are not entering

Seeing Into Eternity

into a very tumultuous time (which I believe that we are) The Order is destined to arise and take the Church higher. I believe that we have yet to see the major events outlined in Revelation but also that we have seen some of the "horse riders" already, IE the white horse, etc.

Timelessness in the Spirit or Being in the Moment with God
Many have experienced the state of timelessness in the spirit. Being in the moment with God is when time not only stands still but time ceases to exist. Prophetically, you stand with Him in heavenly places, and time does not even apply. You exist on earth, and you are in heaven.

re: Timelessness and Travel

The Lord is showing me that timelessness is the key to the kingdom and the key to the Key of David and the key to Melchizedek. (See Becoming Melchizedek Book II, Unto Fullness, the "Key of David" section in Chapter 3: Philadelphia Coming Forth.) David stepped out of time and into eternity/timelessness regularly when he wrote his psalms. The high priest activated timelessness when the blood was applied to the mercy seat on the Ark of the Covenant, and the ark traveled back in time to when there was no sin of the people. That is how God did not merely roll back their sins but made the sins as if they never happened because they never happened. Jesus also operated outside of time when He said that He only spoke what He heard the Father speak and only did what He saw the Father doing. (Paraphrase of John 5:19-20.) Jesus was collocated in heaven and on earth at the same time. So, shall it be with God's Priests. The Priests can stand at the edge of eternity and see either backward or forward. Time is a circular continuum for us We can see the ancient of days on His throne. We can see the twenty-four elders and the living creatures. We hear and see what is going on in the throne room, and we move with the ebb and flow as God the Father continues to create both in the heaven, the heavens or celestial realms and on the earth. All creation is progressive and never stops. God constantly builds upon what was just created or what was just enacted. Ian Clayton tells us that the high priest activated timelessness when the blood was applied to the mercy seat on the Ark of the Covenant, and the ark traveled back in time to when there was no sin of the people.

That is how God did not merely roll back their sins but made the sins as if they never happened because they never happened.

The Order can also move forward in time.
When God shows you an event from the past or future he is actually taking you to that time in the spirit and this is actually time travel. Put even more accurately, it is spiritual travel beyond the realm of time.

Have you been able to stop things from happening even when the enemy tries to change things? Daniel 7:25 CJB says of satan, *"He will try to exhaust the holy ones of the Most High. He will attempt to alter the seasons and the law."* When the enemy finds willing vessels and tries things before God has ordained them, The Order will move ahead in time with the help of the angels and the seven Spirits of God and the holy ones and stop him. As I stated before, heaven is going to train us. We will eventually come of full age when we can do these things ourselves, but until then we need heavenly assistance. For example, I see an angel able to open up a window in time so we can not only see what has or will happen but also so we can step into this window or portal and into a time or season in heaven, the heavens, or on the earth. Sometimes we will even see into hell.

How did Jesus go into the bowels of hell and preach deliverance to the captives? How did He bring all the Old Testament saints back with Him to heaven? I see that He stepped into one of these portals. Was Jesus actually consigned to hell for three days in the grave? My opinion is that He had the freedom to come and go between heaven and hell. (See Matthew 12:40.)

We are heading into a season where if you can believe it, you can have it. Mountains will move into the sea. (See Mark 11:23.) If you can see it in the spirit realm for the future, you can pull it into the present. This ability is true time travel, and all true time travel is spiritual.

Ask the Lord to help you move forward in time. Seek this gifting so that you can make the right decisions now and not make a mistake or waste your time. The right spouse for your child, the right employee to hire, the right place to live, etc. Ask, "Lord, if I live here what will happen? Show me the future." Exercise these abilities. *"But strong meat belongeth to them that are of full age, even those who by reason of use have their senses exercised to discern both good and evil."* (Hebrews 5:14 KJV) Try it, you'll like it. I say this for myself as well. Through WISE, we will be developing spiritual exercises on how to do this and more. As the Lord teaches me as Melchizedek so will I teach you. However, even now you have the Holy Spirit: *"You don't really need a human teacher. You know that his Spirit teaches you about all things."* (1 John 2:27 PHILLIPS.)

Tasting the Powers of the Age to Come

Hebrews 6:5 TLB refers to *"the mighty powers of the world to come."* We had better stop referring to these powers as powers of the age to come as today we are bringing the age to come into *our* age and time and space. The age to come, the final restoration of all things, began as I've said, in 2012. (See more on the Mayan calendar and 2012 under the Dominion section in Chapter 5: The Purpose of Melchizedek.) (See also "Advanced Powers" under Chapter 3: Prophets, Apostles, *and* Kings 2.0 in *Becoming Melchizedek Book II, Unto Fullness.*)

Portals

A portal is like Jacob's ladder in Genesis 28:10-17. The Patriarch Jacob was running from his brother Esau, and in need of rest, he laid his head on a rock. There he saw in an open vision a ladder with angels going up and down on it. Furthermore, the Lord was standing at the top of the ladder. Jacob named the place Bethel or House of God. He was astonished, and exclaimed, "How awesome is this place." A portal is a kind of hole that has been punched into the spiritual realm allowing heaven and the heavenly beings free access back and forth to earth. Through a portal, they can operate without any hindrance. A portal is an open heaven. And portals exist today. Moravian Falls, NC is such a portal, and so is Redding, CA where Bill Johnson's Bethel Church is.

Through our holy lives we will allow portals for the angels to freely enter our reality. Thus in a sense we will bring to earth those now in the throne room of the Father—the seraphim, cherubim, the watchers, the elders, the holy ones, etc.

We will become tour guides of the earth for them, and we will utilize portals so heaven can come to earth.

The dark kingdom has its portals, too. Many believe that the CERN scientists, of the European Organization for Nuclear Research near France, are meddling in areas they know little about. The dial-up in 2015 of acceleration power in the hundreds of gigahertz range could potentially open up a black hole that could consume the earth. CERN, through particle acceleration, is trying to beam beings, likely evil, from other dimensions to earth. Hell's forces, positioned under the earth, also want to invade earth. The separations from the interdimensional are being torn through in this very hour. Beings out of Hell are trying to alter the natural state and separation of things. However, heaven will be ready. We, as Melchizedek, are right on time in our training. As I stated earlier, even though all hell is about to break loose, these dark forces don't stand a chance. They know it. God knows it. And we will experience it as The Priests of the Lord.

Because we have paid the price of humility and debasement, we will be the ones to help God's heavenly visitors come to earth to gain the authority in the earth realm necessary for us to reign and rule as true shepherds over God's people.

Breaking through Death

In Matthew 5:10 KJV, Jesus said to pray, *"Thy kingdom come."* And the truth is that the breaking in of the kingdom in fullness is progressive. The experience of the eternal kingdom is happening for some saints in greater measure than it is happening for others. Melchizedek believers, as leading edge saints, are pursuing the kingdom in fullness with the promise or prospect of being those who do break through the veil separating the realm of time and the eternal. (See Hebrews 6:19-20.) One day, we will break through death itself.

Amalgamation of Heaven and Earth

The Melchizedek Order will bring the alignment, or agreement and alliance, of heaven and earth into perfect unity and balance.

At times, it will seem like there is almost no difference between the atmosphere of heaven and the atmosphere of earth. An amalgamation shall be.

Rapture

Many were looking for the rapture of the church on Sunday, September 13th, 2015—the day of the Feast of Trumpets. I am sorry, but the great "catching away" did not happen on this date. But the Lord does have something to say about this Feast, a type of God's final call to mankind. God, and specifically the Father, is going to tabernacle with His people again. God is not only coming down here, but we, His true church, are going up where He is. Consider the Scripture 1 Thessalonians 4:16-17 KJV,

> *For the Lord himself shall descend from heaven with a shout, with the voice of the archangel, and with the trump of God: and the dead in Yeshua shall rise first: Then we which are alive and remain shall be caught up together with them in the clouds, to meet the Lord in the air: and so shall we ever be with the Lord.*

Saints, let's meet the Lord in the air. A meeting shall happen below heaven and above earth. The church needs to learn to ascend and meet heaven as it descends. Also, the church must work by God's plan and His standards and under heaven's requirements. Heaven has opened a door and *is* requiring us to *"come up here."* Again see Revelation 4:1.

This verse is not merely about the traditional understanding of the rapture of the church though it may cause a *rupture* in the church. Instead, it's also an opening or invitation to the amalgamation of heaven and earth. An amalgamation happens when two distinct elements come together and form as one. The idea is that the two are better and stronger than the one.

An Appointment for Amalgamation Work
In dental work an amalgam is the fusing of mercury that is a liquid at room temperature with gold or silver. The gold is soft and malleable. When the gold combines with mercury, it forms a malleable but hard and stable metal that is used to make crowns. God wants to bring us forth as an amalgamation work with Himself—a union with His nature.

"Out of the abundance of the heart, the mouth speaks," Jesus instructs in Matthew 12 and Luke 6. God wants to repair our broken teeth in our mouths so to speak and clean up the words that we have been speaking. There are cracks, cavities, and bad roots in need of repair, even at the foundation of our beings. These need covering by His crowns—His crowning glory.

I see a golden crown in the mouth of God's children empowering you to speak. This crown helps to shape the air that is coming out of the mouth and helps the mouth and the tongue to form words. You need to speak with God's breath flowing over new golden teeth. A new golden message from heaven will flow through you—one that replaces the old, cracked, rotten and even painful "toothache" of a message. Even to be replaced is the old message spoken by some that God is going to take us out, rapture us, before anything really challenging happens on earth.

Amalgamation is where we are headed—meeting God, getting His mandates, and speaking them. Amalgamation will bring a change in our confession.

Dual Action

As heaven's resources, abilities from Above, wisdom and power from On High come to us in the air or spiritual realm, our ministry will not just be earthly or terrestrial. The church must awaken and arise/ascend to meet Him in the air. There is a dual action here. Heaven will no longer do all the work. God the Father has already sent Yeshua (Jesus) for salvation. Jesus has already sent the Spirit of the Father (the Holy Spirit) for the Baptism in the Spirit. Now, all of heaven is reaching out in the atmosphere above the earth. This atmosphere of earth is going to be combined or amalgamated with the atmosphere of heaven. All of heaven will not truly descend until the New Jerusalem city descends at the start of the Millennial Reign of Yeshua. But what *is* about to happen is heaven working with the church on earth in selected territories and regions all over. This joining of forces is the next step in the process of *"Thy kingdom come."*

Bear in mind that Lucifer is called "the Prince of the Power of the Air." (Ephesians 2:2 KJV.) Together, heaven and earth are now challenging His reign in this space. The air above the earth is the space between heaven and earth. It's a space of positional reigning and ruling with Yeshua in heavenly Places. (Ephesians 2:6.) God will set up some heavenly Places as portals between heaven and earth. Will your home be such a place? Your work? Your church? It is up to you. I believe via such spaces the rapture of the church will eventually take place. Dr. Bill Hamon calls this "R/T" or Resurrection/Translation space. The amalgamation before us has to do with heaven's authority in earth and kingly and priestly duties to be administered by The Order of Melchizedek Priests. (For more see *Becoming Melchizedek Book II, Unto Fullness*, the "Advanced Powers" section of Chapter 3: Apostles, Prophets, *and* Kings 2.0.)

Chapter 12: Melchizedek Manifested

As the Melchizedek Order manifests on earth, many Biblical truths and anointing's will also come to the fore in fullness. We will know the Godhead within. The Father will be with us as He was with Yeshua. We will know Garden of Eden realities: *"the Lord God walking* (and talking with us) *in the garden in the cool of the day."* (Genesis 3:8 KJV.) Ordinary believers will rise to carry prophet, priest, and king mantles. Elijah's and Elisha's will arise. Certain "fathers" will be like Moses. And companies of those with Joseph and Daniel callings will have strategic roles.

The Godhead Within: An Impenetrable Fortress

God, the Father, wants to manifest Himself to you and me within. He desires to establish Himself as an impenetrable fortress inside our bodies or temples—impenetrable as far as the enemy. We need this safety and protection and resilience for the days that are coming. Even now we need the Father as our fortress. We will be the "box" or the living Ark of the Covenant. Multitudes of us.

Back to the Garden

The habitation of God among men will be as it was originally in the garden. Yeshua and Holy Spirit have been sent already, but now the Father has come back to dwell with men on the earth in a manifest way. The Apostolic hubs now in development may serve as places where God will tabernacle with us. But these places will be especially found wherever Melchizedek Priests operate. This establishment of the manifest presence of God will be followed by the physical return of Yeshua—His second coming.

The Restoration of the Three Mantles

Believers *will* walk in the three traditional mantles or functions of prophet, priest, and king as Melchizedek comes. These basic mantles are precursors and prerequisites to fulfilling the Melchizedek Priesthood. Melchizedek will operate in any or all of these as well and then some. (For more on the apostolic and five-fold mantles that Melchizedek Priests will walk in as well as those of prophet, priest, and king, see Chapter 7: Functions of the Melchizedek Order in *Becoming Melchizedek Book I, Foundations.*)

Elijah/Elisha Acts of Power

Elijah/Elisha works of miraculous power will be released. We can expect stadium gatherings with acts of great power among us. The church will humiliate the enemy. God will give the type of strategic intelligence employed by Elisha and outlined in II Kings 5 and 6. You may recall that Elisha predicted the Syrians every move. He exhibited unparalleled prophetic accuracy, and so will we. Purity of heart and motive and deed are coming to the Body—Melchizedek first. Melchizedek will work with the seraphim to purify God's church as noted in Chapter 8: The Church and Her Melchizedek. Rebukes will come to the apostate church; wisdom will come to the obedient. And Luke 1:17 KJV will soon begin to happen, *"And he shall go before him in the spirit and power of Elias, to turn the hearts of the fathers to the children, and the disobedient to the wisdom of the just; to make ready a people prepared for the Lord."*

Moses' Apostolic Fatherhood

As Melchizedek is manifested, Christ like leadership will arise. And true apostolic ministry with wise and true spiritual fathering behind it will exist in the church. As Moses was a father to Israel so will the end-time fathers lead and father the church. Authority and delegation of authority will happen in an orderly way as the Lord's army takes shape under Melchizedek leadership. Remember, these will be apostles but with an augmented prophetic and kingly and priestly ministry. Acts of deliverance will be forthcoming for God's people. True Priests will counter the New Age counterfeits. Of course, we can expect national judgments, too. As we *"ask for wisdom,"* we will have it. (See James 1:5 TLB.)

The Joseph and Daniel Companies

The Josephs and the Daniels will be sources of provision for believers in the days coming. Men and women with these anointing's will carry authority and shoulder responsibility in the business and governmental mountains. Josephs and Daniels will be pursuers of purity and godly character. Their hearts will undergo the longest times of purification by God because of the great finances they will handle. These companies will be distributors of the wealth of the wicked to God's called ones. (See Proverbs 13:22.) God will endow His Josephs and Daniels with a spirit of excellence. They will be global problem solvers, project managers, engineers, and handlers of national resources. Wisdom will be *"the principle thing"* to them. (See Proverbs 4:7.)

Melchizedek Manifested

Chapter 13: Resources: the Meat of Melchizedek

Melchizedek Comes By Revelation

You might ask, "Charles, can you prove what you are saying by the Word?" In this work, much *has* already been proven in the Word, but much will have to be borne out by experience that what I am saying about the rise of The Order is the truth. And The Order will have to start operating in the fashion that I have foretold. Also, I recommend a few other books on Melchizedek to add to your foundation. (See the Resources section in this chapter.) I am giving the next level of what the Lord has for The Order in *Becoming Melchizedek Book II, Unto Fullness*. Both of my Melchizedek books build upon some of what has been already written by others. Both project into the future and include prophetic predictions.

The future will either bear out what I have written or not. I have been faithful to the heavenly vision, and that's all we can do as His servants and friends. Habakkuk 2:2 KJV instructs visionaries like me, *"And the LORD answered me, and said, Write the vision, and make it plain upon tables, that he may run that readeth it."*

The Qumran Vantage Point

As we come to the end of *Book I Foundations*, let's take a look at what the Qumran people thought about Melchizedek.

Melchizedek and the Dead Sea Scrolls
Three short posts from the February 2009 Christian Monthly Standard follow with my comments.

"Melchizedek and the Dead Sea Scrolls"
by Brent Kercheville

One of the fascinating things I found from reading the Dead Sea Scrolls is the number of references to Melchizedek. There are 11 mentions of Melchizedek in the scrolls, a curiosity due to the limited information given about him in Genesis 14. Understanding how the Jews thought of Melchizedek colors our understanding of what the writer of Hebrews is arguing concerning Melchizedek in Hebrews 7. So I thought I would post some of the Qumran references to Melchizedek for others to consume. The [. . .] indicates broken text because the fragment is lost or damaged and cannot be translated.

11Q13 2:2-10

2:2 And concerning what Scripture says, "In [this] year of Jubilee [you shall return, every one of you, to your property" (Leviticus 25:13) and what is also written, "And this]

3 is the [ma]nner of [the remission:] every creditor shall remit the claim that is held [against a neighbor, not exacting it of a neighbor who is a member of the community, because God's] remission [has been proclaimed" (Deuteronomy 15:2.)]

4 [The interpretation] is that it applies [to the L]ast Days and concerns the captives, just as [Isaiah said: "To proclaim the Jubilee to the captives" (Isaiah 61:1.) ... just] as

5 [...] and from the inheritance of Melchizedek, f[or ... Melchize]dek, who

6 will return them to what is rightfully theirs. He will proclaim to them the Jubilee, thereby releasing th[em from the debt of a]ll their sins. [He shall pro]claim this decree

7 in the fir[s]t [wee]k of the Jubilee period that foll[ows nine j]ubilee periods. Then the "D[ay of Atone]ment" shall follow af[ter] the [te]nth [ju]bilee period,

8 when he shall atone for all the Sons of [Light] and the peopl[e who are pre]destined to Mel[chi]zedek. [...] upo[n the]m [...] For

9 this is the time decreed for "the year of Melchiz[edek]'s favor" (Isaiah 61:2, modified), [and] by his might he w[i]ll judge God's holy ones and so establish a righteous ki[n]gdom, as it is written

10 about him in the Songs of David, "A godlike being has taken his place in the council of God; in the midst of the divine beings he holds judgment" (Psalm 82:1).

The Melchizedek figure is pictured in combination with the year of Jubilee. Jubilee was the forgiveness of debts. But the Qumran community saw this Melchizedek figure as doing more than forgiving debts, but also forgiving sins (2:6). Not only this,

178

Resources: the Meat of Melchizedek

Melchizedek is placed on the same level as God. In referencing Isaiah 61:2, the Qumran community substituted "the year of the Lord's favor" for "the year of Melchizedek's favor" (2:9). Further, Melchizedek would establish a righteous kingdom and will judge the holy ones (2:9).

The Qumran people saw Melchizedek as a divine Messianic figure who would establish a kingdom and release the people of their debt to sin. It seems their concept of the Messiah was not farfetched. But it is curious that they equated Melchizedek to this work. Perhaps this is the reason for the argument found in Hebrews 7 that Melchizedek was superior because he held the office of priest and king simultaneously. So the Messiah would do the same.

Scholars debate over how influential the Qumran community was in Judaism from the second century BC to the first century AD. They also debate over how reflective their beliefs were to that of the rest of Jewish society. Were they just a small group in the wilderness with strange beliefs? If so, many of the documents like the Copper Scroll do not make much sense. Or did the Qumran community have the same general beliefs and doctrinal ideas as the rest of the Jewish population, but lived in the wilderness either because they perceived the nation and priesthood to be defiled and/or because of the approaching invasion of the Roman armies?

[Charles Robinson: Melchizedek will return to them what is rightfully theirs. He shall declare to them the Jubilee and release them from all their sins. (This the New Testament power to forgive or remit sins from John 20:23.) He has the power to release finances and clear from debt. He (Yeshua as Melchizedek) shall atone for the Sons of Light and the people that are predestined to Melchizedek. These happenings are of the time of Melchizedek's favor (from Isaiah 61). He will judge God's holy ones and establish the kingdom. A godlike being has taken his place in the council of God; in the midst of the divine beings he holds judgment. Wow, this is exciting!]

Below is more about the Qumran people's belief in what Melchizedek would do:

11Q13

2:10 Scripture also s[ays] about him, "Over [it]
2:11 take your seat in the highest heaven; A divine being will judge the peoples" (Psalm 7:7—8). Concerning what Scripture s[ays, "How long will y]ou judge unjustly, and sh[ow] partiality to the wick[e]d? [S]el[ah" (Psalm 82:2),]
2:12 the interpretation applies to Belial and the spirits predestined to him, becau[se all of them have rebe]lled, turn[ing] from God's precepts [and so becoming utterly wicked.]
2:13 Therefore Melchizedek will thoroughly prosecute the veng[ea]nce required by Go[d's] statu[te]s. [Also, he will deliver all the captives from the power of B]elial, and from the power of all [the spirits predestined to him.]

In the last post, we noticed that Melchizedek was considered to be a divine Messianic being who would deliver the people from their sins and debts. In this excerpt, we also learn that this divine Messianic figure called Melchizedek would judge the people. Particularly, he will execute vengeance against those who have rebelled against God's precepts. Also, he will deliver all who are captive under the power of satan (Belial).

In our final look at how Melchizedek was perceived by the Qumran community, consider this excerpt about Melchizedek:

> 11Q13
>
> 14 Allied with him will be all the ["righteous] divine beings" (Isaiah 61:3). [The ...] is that wh[ich ... al]l the divine beings. This vi[sitation]
>
> 15 is the Day of [Salvation] that He has decreed [through Isai]ah the prophet [concerning all the captives,] inasmuch as Scripture sa[ys, "How] beautiful
>
> 16 upon the mountains are the fee[t of] the messeng[er] who [an]nounces peace, who brings [good] news, [who announces salvat]ion, who [sa]ys to Zion, 'Your [di]vine being [reigns'"] (Isaiah 52:7).]
>
> 17 This Scripture's interpretation: "the mounta[ins" are the] prophet[s,] they w[ho were sent to proclaim God's truth and to] proph[esy] to all I[srael.]
>
> 18 "The messenger" is the [An]ointed of the spir[it,] of whom Dan[iel] spoke, ["After the sixty-two weeks, an Anointed one shall be cut off" (Daniel 9:26). The "messenger who brings]
>
> 19 good news, who announ[ces salvation"] is the one of whom it is wri[tt]en, ["to proclaim the year of the Lord's favor, the day of vengeance of our God;]

20 to comfo[rt all who mourn" (Isaiah 61:2). This Scripture's interpretation:] he is to inst[r]uct them about all the periods of history for eter[nity ... and in the statutes of]

21 [the] truth. [...]

22 [... dominion] that passes from Belial and ret[urns to the Sons of Light ...]

23 [...] by the judgment of God, just as it is written concerning him, ["who says to Zi]on 'Your divine being reigns'" (Isaiah 52:7). ["Zi]on" is

24 [the congregation of all the sons of righteousness, who] uphold the covenant and turn from walking [in the way] of the people. "Your di[vi]ne being" is

25 [Melchizedek, who will del[iv[er them from the po]wer of Belial.

All of the righteous beings will be aligned with Melchizedek, this divine Messiah. The Qumran community continues by quoting a number of Messianic Scripture and ties them to Melchizedek. In verse 16 of this scroll we see the phrase "Your divine being reigns." This phrase also appears in verse 23 of the scroll. Jump down to verses 24-25 we read that Melchizedek is the divine being who will deliver them from the power of Satan (Belial).

Further, Melchizedek seems to be described as the Anointed One, another Messianic reference. The "messenger" is also referring to Melchizedek, not only because the context is about the understanding of this Messianic figure, but also because of verse 19 of the scroll. Recall that the quotation "to proclaim the year of the Lord's favor" was applied to Melchizedek. We noticed this fact in the first post where Qumran community adapted the Isaiah passage to read, "to proclaim the year of Melchizedek's favor."

Parallels with the Teachings of Jesus

Multiple Scriptures show how these same Qumran concepts were taught about Jesus. I think we can readily see the parallels with Jesus. Certainly, Jesus is the high priest after The Order of Melchizedek as Hebrews 7 continues this useful parallel. The Qumran people's expectation of Melchizedek is very much fulfilled in the activities and character of Jesus. He, Melchizedek, is a divine being who will judge the peoples from the highest heavens. He will also judge evil beings with the vengeance of our God. (And it's noteworthy that this reads like Isaiah 61:2.)

The Need for Meat or Solid Food

There *is* a need to understand the original audience, original background, and context when we read the Scripture. Melchizedek clearly has a fuller, deeper concept in the Jewish mind in the first century than we understand. The more background and history we are able to understand, the better and more appropriately we can understand and apply the Scripture. This belief system concerning Melchizedek reminds us of what the writer of Hebrews 5:9-11 ESV said, *"And being made perfect, he became the source of eternal salvation to all who obey Him, being designated by God a high priest after The Order of*

Melchizedek. About this we have much to say, and it is hard to explain, since you have become dull of hearing."

Was it not this symbolism concerning Melchizedek that the writer of Hebrews wanted to discuss, but was unable to because of the spiritual laziness and dullness of hearing that these people had? May we not be spiritually dull and lazy so that we will seek greater depths of knowledge in the Word of God on Melchizedek and all that is ahead..

Let's continue with Hebrews 5:12-14 ESV:

> *For though by this time you ought to be teachers, you need someone to teach you again the basic principles of the oracles of God. You need milk, not solid food, for everyone who lives on milk is unskilled in the word of righteousness, since he is a child. But solid food is for the mature, for those who have their powers of discernment trained by constant practice to distinguish good from evil.*

The writer of Hebrews, whom I believe was Paul the Apostle, said that there was a lot more to say about Melchizedek. Think about this! But, he notes that the readers were dull of hearing and digressing from meat back to milk. Melchizedek is a meaty topic and that is why you are reading this book—because you want more than the simple teachings on The Priesthood. You want the deep things of God. Hopefully, I am satisfying your hunger and thirst for righteousness and serving you a good and well-balanced meal chock-full of vitamins and minerals and sides of revelation with the bread of inspiration— that you can become Melchizedek.

Recommendation: do buy and read *Becoming Melchizedek Book II, Unto Fullness* for vision and equipping for the next level in Melchizedek Priesthood life. Also prayerfully consider applying for membership in Melchizedek International under WISE Ministries International. The application is in the Appendix to *Foundations Book I*.

Final note: If you have been involved with Mormonism or the New Age or witchcraft or Satanism, and my books have touched you, or if you have given your life to Yeshua or are considering this, I want to know. You can email me at charles@melchizedek.international. First of all, you need to find other believers that believe like us in your area because it is so important to have fellowship. I am conducting Kingdom Church services every Sunday either in Southern California or in China.

Charles Robinson

Recommended Resources

Melchizedek the New Millennium Priesthood
by Nita (LaFond) Johnson 2008
A classic book which established the foundation for my Melchizedek books
http://worldforjesus.org

The Order of Melchizedek: Rediscovering the Eternal Priesthood of Jesus Christ and How It Affects Us Today
By Dr. Francis Myles 2008
http://francismyles.com

Back to the Melchizedek Future an *Expose of the Forgotten*
By Dr. David L. Perry, Th. D.
2013. A very detailed and well researched book

Ian Clayton's several Melchizedek recordings. Available on www.sonofthunder.org

The ministry of Dr. Stephen Jones. See GKM's Daily Web Logs
God's Kingdom Ministries

WISE Books/School for Melchizedek Forthcoming
The Melchizedek Prophet
The Melchizedek Apostle
Melchizedek Devotional

Seven Mountain Melchizedek: Melchizedek Strategies in the Seven Mountains

Seven Mountains University — *online school*

Melchizedek International

(See also *Becoming Melchizedek Book II, Unto Fullness* Chapter 12: Resources for Melchizedek's Pursing Fullness.)

APPENDIX A: Application to Melchizedek International

If you feel the call to become a priest in The Order after having read *Foundations* and *Unto Fullness*, please submit the application for commissioning below. We do not use the term ordination and prefer to use the word commissioning. God has already ordained you but man commissions you (sends you forth for a specific purpose). You definitely should read *Book II, Unto Fullness* before or during the application process. An online version of the application is here.

There is a $25.00 application fee as well as a $495.00 (minimum) yearly administrative fee. You can pay the application and the yearly dues here. Yearly membership dues include a one hour consult with Charles. Additionally, you are required to send us an update on your ministry progress quarterly and to attend one of our Tipping Point and/or a Melchizedek events at least once per year.

Please scan and email the application to charles@Melchizedek.International.

Becoming Melchizedek Foundations

Melchizedek International

<u>Application for Membership</u>

PERSONAL INFORMATION

Organization and/or Individual or Couple Name(s):

_____

_____

_____

Date: _____/_____/_____

Street Address:
_____

City:
_____

State: _____ Zip: _____

Email: _____

Phone: (____) _____

Cell Phone (____) _____

Date Saved _____/_____/_____

Birth Date _____/_____/_____

Date Water Baptized _____/_____/_____

Date Spirit Filled _____/_____/_____

APPENDIX A

Occupation (Please state if student)

_____

_____

Hours worked or studied/in classes per week: _____

Church Member? Yes or No? ____ (If yes, name of church)

_____

Address _____

City _____ State _____ Zip _____

In which departments of the ministry are you involved?

_____

Please provide your pastor's names:

_____

_____

_____

Reasons why you are seeking membership in MI?

_____

_____

_____

_____

EDUCATIONAL BACKGROUND:

Schooling completed:

_____

_____

Degrees in?

_____

_____

Other training or specializations:

_____

_____

What were the most important things you learned about life in your educational environment?

_____

_____

_____

_____

If applicable, PROPHETIC MINISTRY TRAINING BACKGROUND:

Trained with what ministry or school or when?

_____

_____

APPENDIX A

_____

_____

_____

What have you learned about the Lord and His people through this training?

_____

_____

_____

_____

_____

If no formal training or experience in the Prophetic Ministry, are you open you open to learn? Yes or No? _____

If applicable, BUSINESS EXPERIENCE IN THE MARKETPLACE:

Describe:
_____

_____

_____

_____

How may this be an asset to the Melchizedek International?

APPENDIX A

Please complete the following sentences:

1-The most important thing to me is:

_____

_____

_____

_____

2-What I do best is:

_____

_____

_____

_____

3-What concerns me about the world is:

_____

4-What makes me upset is:

_____

_____

5-My biggest accomplishments were:

_____

_____

6-My personality is best described as:

_____

_____

7-What makes me most happy is:

_____

8-Jesus Yeshua is:

_____

_____

9-Prayer is:

_____

_____

10-What people like about me is:

_____

11-God to me is:

_____

_____

12-What makes me feel most at peace is:

_____

APPENDIX A

13-The Word of God is:

_____

_____

Will you be seeking certification? and/or commissioning?

Yes____ No ____

Will you be seeking commissioning?

Yes___ No ____

Please send me more information on the following tracks:

    Melchizedek   _____

    Intercession   _____

    Coaching   _____

    Licensing/Ordination   _____

Do you have any history in the area of intercession?

Yes or No _____

If Yes, INTERCESSION HISTORY:

(List individual & group intercession only to the extent that you can do so without violating confidentiality)

<u>Intercession for/with Whom?</u>

<u>Dates?</u>

_____

_____

_____

_____

<u>Current?</u>

_____

_____

<u>Describe:</u>

_____

_____

_____

_____

APPENDIX A

Previous:

_____
_____

Describe:

_____
_____
_____
_____

If known, please check which spiritual gifts you operate in according to 1 Corinthians 12:4-12.
Note: This experience is NOT a requirement for membership.

Word of Wisdom	_____
Word of Knowledge	_____
Faith	_____
Gifts of Healing	_____
Working of Miracles	_____
Prophecy	_____
Discerning of Spirits	_____
Tongues	_____
Interpretation of Tongues	_____

Please describe:

_____
_____
_____
_____

If applicable, PROPHETIC MINISTRY HISTORY (*only to the extent that you can do so without violating confidentiality*)

Giving Prophetic Ministry Where?
Dates?

_____
_____
_____

Current:

_____
_____

Describe:

_____
_____
_____

APPENDIX A

Previous:

_____

_____

Describe:

_____

_____

_____

_____

If applicable, LIFE/SPIRITUAL COACHING HISTORY (*only to the extent that you can do so without violating confidentiality*)

Coaching for/with Whom?

Dates?

Current?

_____

_____

Describe:

_____

_____

_____

_____

Becoming Melchizedek Foundations

Previous:

_____

_____

Describe:

_____

_____

_____

If applicable, CHAPLAINCY and/or COUNSELOR HISTORY (*only to the extent that you can do so without violating confidentiality*)
Coaching for/with Whom?

_____

_____

_____

Address:

_____

_____

Phone #:

APPENDIX A

Dates:

Current:

Describe:

Previous:

Describe:

_____

_____

_____

_____

If applicable, CHURCH SERVICE HISTORY:

Name of Church

_____

Dates

_____

Current:

_____

Describe:

_____

_____

_____

_____

APPENDIX A

Previous:

_____

_____

Describe:

_____

_____

_____

_____

PERSONAL REFERENCES

List two personal references (not including relatives) with telephone numbers.

Name:

_____

Phone:

_____

Email:

_____

Becoming Melchizedek Foundations

Name:

_____

Phone:

_____

Email:

_____

The information I have given in this application is correct and complete to the best of my knowledge. I understand that false information or significant omissions may disqualify me from further consideration for membership.

By signing below, I give permission to MI to contact my references and permission to my references to speak freely about me with the MI.

Should my application be accepted, I agree to the terms and conditions of membership and to refrain from activities that are illegal or unethical as they especially relate to the code of ethics and conduct of the MI. I understand that membership in MI is not an offer for or guarantee of employment and that MI is an educational and professional organization.

APPENDIX A

I also understand that MI makes no warranties of any kind, either to members or to any third parties.

Applicant's Signature:

_____

Date:

____/____/____

© 2015, Melchizedek International

APPENDIX B: 7 MOUNTAINS PROPHECIES 2015

By Dr. Charles Robinson

Copyright © 2014 WISE Ministries International

Subjects for the words below: Gamma Ray Burst, Your Tale, Our Tale, Starburst, Angels Bursting onto the Scene, Becoming Melchizedek, 5775, USA Politics, Church, Lawlessness, The Prophetic Ministry in 2015, China, USA Defense, Family Survival Plan, Shields of Defense, Russia and Ukraine and Others, Israel, Oil, Housing, Gold and Silver, Foreign Policy, Illuminati, Media, Arts and Entertainment, Family, Business, Education, and Exposure of Corruption.

BURSTING ONTO THE SCENE IN 2015!

To burst onto the scene means to become suddenly famous. Our God is going to become suddenly famous. So will many of you — in heaven for sure and maybe even on earth! Read on!

A Gamma-ray burst. These are the brightest electromagnetic events that occur in the universe. See Gamma-ray burst for more on the science of these bursts of activity from other worlds.

The word for 2015 that the Lord has given me is "*Burst*." There will be a burst of activities, a burst of new inventions, a burst of new cures, bursts of angelic activity such as we have not seen in many decades. Thus new opportunities for God's people. I will burst on the scene with the new for you, and you will burst onto the scene in 2015, says the Lord! The Lord says I am not going to hold back this year. I am going to let the cat out of the bag. He is not a pussycat; He is the lion of the tribe of Judah! Some surprises are in store, and more things will be uncovered—both good and not so good. But ultimately, this is for my purposes for this nation and the nations of the world. A GRB, or gamma-ray burst, occurs from other worlds (or other galaxies) and emits enough energy in the form of ultra-violet, optical, X-ray, microwave and radio waves in a few seconds to a few minutes to exceed the entire output of our sun over its lifetime. God is coming in 2015 with *His EMP's:* what I call "HEMPs" (His Electro-Magnetic pulses). Of course not cannabis hemp but HEMP from the Most High—from *His* world into *ours* on *many wavelengths. His pulses are coming suddenly* with some bursts of spiritual activity and helps for humanity. Especially help for His church. Now is not the time of the Antichrist, nor is it the time for World War III. God is coming into 2015 to *intervene*. The GRB waves are used in *all sorts of communications* in our world. Likewise, God wants to communicate with us in many new ways in 2015 with His bursts of *impulses and messages* to mankind! *This message I am delivering to you today,* New Year's Eve 2014, *is about the messages* that will come. I see the word *burst* relating to sudden surprises and solutions and new opportunities for you. It's like a flower suddenly opening with all of its beauty just appearing seemingly out of nowhere. But it's beauty was prepared in the bud all along and came from the

APPENDIX B

bud. You are in the bud and the bud has been in the environment and atmosphere that I have prepared you in, says the Lord! Your environment has been for your good.

Also, like the way a skyrocket on the 4thof July enters the darkness of night and eyes strain to see its path, as higher and higher she goes, it's like your friends and family are saying, "We know God is going to do *something* with her…." Then *suddenly* a burst of activity happens, and the night sky is filled with the sight and sound and color in the shape of a beautiful flower. *You are that flower, and God has written your name in the night sky.* You are as permanent a part of the night sky as His stars, solar systems and galaxies! It is time for you to burst onto the scene with the gifts and callings, ideas and creativity that God has placed in the shell or the bud of you. He has been propelling you into the night, streaking you across the skies with almost an unseen tail until the time of your appearing to get you positioned. Now in 2015, you will burst onto the scene and light up the night sky! Daniel 12:3 says that they are wise shall shine like the brightness of the firmament.

YOUR TALE

Like a skyrocket or a comet, it's time for your tail to be seen and your tale to be told. The story of you! It's even time for you to write and get your story out to the world. 2015 is an unprecedented year for writing the book of your life for God's people. God has a Book of Life which records the names of those saved. Why not a book of *your* life story? The story of how He saved you? The story that *became* you—who you are in 2015.

Talk about a coming-out party that will declare your independence from the world systems and celebrate and empower you in this season of independence in *your* sphere of influence around your clients, those you minister to, and those that even will *pay* you for what you know! Liberty is coming! Yes, your knowledge and experience is worthy of payment to you. Think of this as your new career with a stream of income for you. Note: have you thought about entering the new and exciting field of coaching? See my website for more on my new Seven Mountains coaching books: *Let Heaven Invade the Seven Mountains of Culture—7M Coaching Certification Guide*, and the quick read, *Become a Seven Mountains Coach*.

OUR TALE

While I am talking about us, as an update, 2014 was a year of expansion for WISE with our association with the Wagner Leadership Institute (WLI), and our joining the HIM Network (Harvest International Ministry). As well it was a year of growing roots in Southern California both in Orange County and in the Los Angeles area. We conducted our first two and a half day Tipping Point Unconference outside of Texas and in Los Angeles in June. God released angels that had never been released before to California, both Los Angeles and Hollywood, to prepare us for what is to come through the Tipping Point. Go

APPENDIX B

to TippingPointHollywood.com for more information. We conducted several Gates2Hollywood.com meetings also. We also conducted several Tipping Point Networking dinners in cities across America. BTW, let me know if you want to bring the river of God to *your* city.

We are now an empty nest at our house as Nathanael, our only son, went off to Pepperdine University in Malibu.

I wrote six books in 2014, received my Doctorate in Theology and another Doctorate in Divinity. I plan on another five books Lord-willing and time permitting in 2015 as God is bringing our ministry to the world and commissioning me to *"write the vision and make it plain."* Go to LetHeavenInvade7M.com for more info. 2015 has been a year of shifting and true marketplace ministry. I worked in traditional ministry and preached and prophesied as well as lead company efforts in the business mountain using my skills gleaned from the last 20 years. WISE expanded with the establishment of a Governmental Spiritual Advisory Team (GSAT) in Washington, DC, and we expanded our ministry in Hollywood and appeared on several Christian TV programs. From our Seven Mountains Institute: The five-volume *Let Heaven Invade the Seven Mountains of Culture* series is becoming our foundational curriculum for our planned three-year Seven Mountains Institute. Go to 7MInstitute.com for more information. I am working on bringing local church services to a global audience of 120 million through leading the Church on the Air arm of *The Way TV*. Also, I am currently focusing on leading the efforts of a Christian health and wellness direct sales company called One Line Group.

I am part of the leadership for a hydrogen-on-demand company called Now Enterprises. Last but not least, I started a full-service publishing company called Spirit-Led Publishing. Go to SpiritLedPublishing.com for more information. We publish masterpieces.

STARBURST

I think of the candy Starburst—a burst of fruity *island* flavors of variety and color is getting ready to happen for you! New environments with "how about an *island attitude"* happening in *your* mouth. You will *"taste and see* that the Lord is good in 2015." And *speak* of my lovingkindness and *testify* of my goodness; see that I have paced you in a *new environment* and with a *new atmosphere* and communicated with you in a new way on a new level and given you a burst of new opportunities and a platform, says the Lord!

ANGELS BURSTING ONTO THE SCENE

Angels are being released now, and their release will increase and accelerate in 2015. These are angels that correspond to the Seven Spirits of God as outlined in Isaiah 11:2. These angels are communicators and miracle workers, and they will prepare God's people and release them into their modern day Joseph and Daniel callings. Release the seven moves of God—one for each mountain in the seven mountains of culture. See my books for more on this topic.

BECOMING MELCHIZEDEK

See Genesis 14, Psalm 110, Hebrews 5, 6, and 7.

In The Order of Melchizedek, the earthly ministry offices of apostle and prophet are combining with the heavenly administrative functions of king and priest. These four functions will now operate through those that have a role as sons in The Order of Melchizedek. The Order's assignment is to bring an amalgamation of heaven and earth. The offices and functions of apostle and prophet will continue to exist but now have been augmented in the Melchizedek Order. Some apostles and prophets have been and will be promoted to the next level in Melchizedek. For those of you who have been sensing and desiring more, it is here—*it is now*. You will know if this is your calling if you have been operating both as an apostle and a prophet in the past. God is now adding priestly and kingly functions to your assignment. That means bringing The Holy One to the seven mountains with their marketplaces. Again, I am talking about ministering and administering God's holiness from heaven into the earth. Coming within the veil emerging as a high priestly function. Reigning and ruling as a king in a kingly function. Making decrees that have the power of life and death. Melchizedek is about *responsibility* and ultimately *co-creating* with God. You will ultimately be able to say to a mountain, "Be removed," and to the sea, "Let a new mountain or island be formed." This is the fullness of what was promised to Adam. It is the fulfillment of what the new age only claims to be—their claim to be God. We are not divine, but we will be participating in His Godhood, so-to-speak, in the cosmos. This priesthood is the highest form and manifestation of sonship in our day. Please see my forthcoming books: Volume 5 of *Let Heaven Invade the Seven Mountains of Culture—7M General's Certification Guide* for advanced principles and techniques for God's emerging generals and *Becoming Melchizedek*. To be published in 2015.

5775

We must overcome the disappointments of the past with their associated delays and ask God to fill these areas of void with a double portion of His presence. As I write this, we are in the Hebraic year 5775 which is a picture of an open window that we can see through (and this is true for 2014-2019 as well). The last digit 5 in 5775 is a picture of a rushing wind blowing through the window. This year is the year of the whirlwind! 5775 and 5776 are also sabbatical years of *rest*. It is God's whirlwind that He is sending to shake us up and to separate us from that which entangles us. God is freeing us from delay and our past disappointments and filling us with Himself.

USA POLITICS

Politicians will try to ram things through the Congress very quickly to avoid scrutiny. We thought this practice was done only under the Democrats and Obama as seen with Obamacare, but no. This is not your normal Republican Congress. Behind the scenes dinners and agreements are happening. Is this the new-normal in politics on both sides of the aisle?

Amnesty by Memoranda: Whether you sympathize with amnesty or not the way this deal was accomplished was unconstitutional. God tells me that President Obama's unconstitutional memoranda, and these were not even by executive order, will eventually be overturned.

USA GOVERNMENT

The next two years are going to be the most dangerous for this nation since the civil war era. The temptation is for President Obama to continue to do what he wants to and not to be reigned-in by the other two branches of government—the legislative and the judicial. Congress and the Senate are the ones who make laws. The president should only execute the laws. We need our elected officials to have some backbone against this overreach. The word again is temptation. Will laws be made because they *can* be made or because they *should* be and done under the construct and defined limits of law and order and the three branches? The spiritual significance of the overreach of the executive branch and the duplicity and minimization of opposing views cannot be overemphasized. It is huge for the nation and future administrations. Our system and our nation hang in the balance. The Fast and Furious and Benghazi scandals, the Affordable Care Act passed without one vote from the other side. Heaven is crying out for justice and will not be mocked. I say that, again, those things that are going on in secret, the secret meetings and pacts, heaven sees them, and heaven will not be mocked. The Lord says that I have not forgotten this nation and its founding fathers. Not to mention the 18 trillion in national debt and counting. Talk about a burst of activity. What message or impulses are *we* sending and what financial burdens are we laying on the next generation? Men have only cared about themselves and their own ideologies and not the needs of next generations. This not caring is the greatest grievance that heaven has against this nation.

Yet, God has a plan, an alternative energy plan, a burst of economic activity plan that will exceed the industrial and informational revolutions. His is a hydrogen plan, an unlimited nonpolluting energy source to save this nation and the world. We must not give up hope. Heaven's plans and Jesus' plans are greater than any plans the Illuminati or our leaders have for America and the nations of the world. II Chron. 7:14. God's plan may also be to allow for a worldwide Jubilee that wipes away all debts and resets the financial systems of the world.

CHURCH

Many people's coverings are beginning to come off. This is a good thing. Last year I saw people moving into many new assignments and also moving geographically, as we did ourselves. Now I see, as it were, people wrapped up as gifts in wrapping paper. The wrapping paper represents their current spiritual coverings, and it's colorful paper with much variety. But it was thin in its manufacture. The wrapping paper would tear easily after some handling. It was not meant to contain you but to present you. Get it, a present, as in a gift? The wrapping paper was covering up the gift or gifts that God's people had in them. The wrapping paper represents denominations or other ministry groups that have served their purpose. God is taking the wraps off and exposing you and your ministry in a new way. It is time for your gifts to come to the fore. The wraps are coming off in 2015. God is letting the cat out of the bag. Get ready for your burst onto the scene and for your exposure to the world bringing the special gifts that you are in your person and the gifts that you possess. Your covering served a purpose for a season, but now it is changing.

LAWLESSNESS

There is a tendency towards more and more lawlessness among the people in leadership and the civilian population in general. The police have become militarized, and the federal government wants to take over local police forces. This takeover must not be allowed to happen. Racial tensions are better in this country, but the enemy and the globalists are trying to reopen wounds that have been healed. Our young people have way too much time on their hands, such idleness is the devil's playground. Let's put them to work businessmen! Now is the best opportunity for the church to go beyond its four walls and make a difference in their communities.

THE PROPHETIC MINISTRY:
The prophetic ministry is changing—it's getting more accurate and getting more subjective depending on who you are and what your response is. The prophetic is less fixed and more variable. Less "words" for groups of people and more for individuals. Less general "words" and more specific ones. God may not speak as much in one season then all-of-a-sudden speak a lot. It is up to us who are prophets to pull on our relationship with God. Also, those receiving prophetic ministry should pull on God. Pull on our relationship with Him for greater understanding. We are not to be as children but as adults. The Prophetic Ministry is finally maturing in 2015. People are going to be living and experiencing the prophetic in a new way. The Lord says, I am going to open heaven in a new way for access to heaven this year, and I am inviting all to come up higher with me. I will stimulate your five spiritual senses and activate your vision in a new way. In a new way, I will pull you up to where I am so that you can see and prophesy not just *in* the earth but

above the earth. You will see, in an *experiential way* that you are "*seated with me in heavenly places far above all principalities and powers.*" It is essential beginning this year that you see and prophesy from *my* perspective—from heaven's perspective because if you speak from earth's perspective you will be too caught up in and affected by what is happening on the earth. And I desire you to be up in heavenly realms with me. Come up and come into your prophetic ministry and experience it in living color and with all of your spiritual senses and bring it back to earth. You will bring some of heaven with you! Such is the prophetic in The Order of Melchizedek, which is *heaven in earth* not just heaven coming down to earth. Credit for the phrase "heaven in earth" is due to Ian Clayton of Son of Thunder Ministries.

CHINA

Many of China's men do not have prospective wives from which to choose. In 2013, a relaxing of the One Child policy allowed couples to have a second child if one of the parents was an only child. God tells me that a *full moratorium* on the One Child Policy is coming. It may be on a year-by-year basis, but it is coming.

USA DEFENSE

The Lord is telling me that there will be some holes discovered in our defense systems whether these are found to be nuclear, cyber security, etc. This discovery will be much bigger than the

2014 Sony incident (which may have been an inside job BTW). Our defenses both at home and abroad will be tested in a greater way. The enemy will be looking for weaknesses, and people that are plants in the homeland may become much more active this year. Intercession is key as always this year. There will need to be more emergency drills and practices so that we will not have "knee-jerk reactions" to surprises as a nation. Contingency plans must be tested this year. In many cases contingency plans need to be developed. We need to avoid the global repercussions of "knee-jerk reactions."

FAMILY SURVIVAL PLAN

More planning needs to be done at the level of the family. Do you have an emergency evacuation plan? Do you have emergency supplies in a backpack that you can take with you? Can you survive for 3-5 days away from home? Can you filter water? Sleep in the cold? Enough said.

SHIELDS OF DEFENSE

God wants to develop shields of defense over major industries, economies, and territories over this nation and the nations of the world. Specific prayer teams will be raised up for each of these areas this year.

RUSSIA AND UKRAINE AND OTHERS

The enemy wants to start World War III, but it is not time. Also, tensions between North and South Korea, India and Pakistan and Iran and Israel all are creating powder kegs. These tensions have the makings of regional conflicts that could become global in nature. We must pray. Russia is a bear that has been cornered through sanctions. Russia needs to determine whether it is a sheep or goat nation. Russia's economy is in free fall. Russia will look for China for help.

ISRAEL

We have already seen a change in approach by the Palestinians in the Synagogue stabbings. Another change in approach is that the Palestinians are increasing pressure on Israel from the UN and through the USA with a political approach. Pray that the USA stand strong with Israel as our own protection from God relies on this stance. Pray for the peace of Jerusalem, the city founded by Shem, the Melchizedek, who met Abraham in the Valley of the Kings.

OIL

Oil prices could go to $40 a barrel. This rise would be good and bad for the USA, bad for Texas, North Dakota, Pennsylvania, and some other states. Will force a scuttling of many oil platforms. Already there are major layoffs and a slowdown in GDP happening in Texas. Texas is much better positioned this time around than this state was in the 1980's when a major recession hit because of the drop in oil prices.

HOUSING

Look for declines in home values in 2015 in most regions and regional home building upticks in some hot areas and slowdowns in housing starts in other regions.

GOLD AND SILVER

As I said last year do not bet against gold. Gold is finishing 2014 almost exactly where it left off at the end of 2013. It will be a volatile year for gold, and much profit can be made. I feel that everyone should own some silver and have some cash on hand in case of emergencies. $1000.00 or so in different denominations should be adequate.

FOREIGN POLICY

There will be far-reaching consequences to foreign policy decisions that have been made in the last few years. In some cases good consequences, but in others not so good. I hear, "the chickens are coming home to roost."

ILLUMINATI

I hear the Illuminati's "Master Plan" is going to be enacted this year, but God already has a response, and it will come from His people to praying in His will for America and the nations against their own plans and will. Try as they may, the Global Elite will not win.

APPENDIX B

MEDIA

God is raising up 24/7 Christian television via satellite. The stations that will not be ostensibly Christian, but will report the truth to the world.

ARTS AND ENTERTAINMENT

Liz and I are assigned to Hollywood. We commissioned 70 people to the Arts and Entertainment Mountain at our Tipping Point Hollywood unconference in June of 2014. Go to TippingPointHollywood.com for more information and the latest prophetic revelation. I hear that Hollywood is "coming of age." To me, that means that Hollywood is growing up and maturing and that these "adolescents" are being purged to bring quality back to Hollywood. That means more Christian and family-oriented films. In 2014, Hollywood figured out what works and what does not work and what the people want—they want quality films and moral stories to watch. As Hollywood's "Year of the Bible" comes to a close, let every year be a year of the Bible.

FAMILY

Like never before the family is under attack. Attack from the most horrendous video games like Grand Theft Auto 5 to the gay agenda breakdown of traditional marriage. God has a response. The Lord says that new organizations that center on the family and the promotion of Biblical family values will begin to spring up in 2015. Like I called Focus on the Family 35+ years ago, I am calling my culture warriors to fight for the family again, says the Lord. Family and marriage will become a rallying call again from godly candidates in 2016 and beyond.

BUSINESS

New opportunities for Kingdom Businesses are here. Do not let fear hold you back my business people. There are new opportunities for you in which to branch. Again, I see the word *burst* and coming a burst of activity for some businesses that are positioned to benefit from new markets and new product and service lines. I hear, if you stand still in 2015 you will lose ground, and that is not my will for you says the Lord. Your business could also burst if you do not have the infrastructure to handle the coming increases of activity so heed this warning. Counteract fear with faith and intimacy with me. I am calling my businesspeople closer to me in 2015. Rededicate your business to me in 2015 so that I may protect it, says the Lord.

Please see my book, *Let Heaven Invade the Seven Mountains of Culture: 7M Leadership Certification Guide* or the very quick read, *Become a Seven Mountains Leader*, for how you can increase in your ascendancy and influence in the seven mountains spheres through the implementation of a Spiritual Advisory Team and other cutting edge strategies. All of my books are available at the 7MInstitute.com for a discount or on Amazon.

APPENDIX B

EDUCATION

The Lord says that people are going to enlist in God's educational army to take back this mountain especially this year. People now realize that under Common Core the government education at our grade schools and middle schools has almost become off limits as an option for Christian parents because of the indoctrination of children with an altered view of US history and other teachings. One little girl was taught that mommies are not teachers and that she could not learn from her mommy! Parents will rise anew and protest against their children being taught things that are ungodly and unpatriotic. I see a move of God at Harvard University in 2015.

EXPOSURE OF CORRUPTION

Corruption is going to be further uncovered in all seven mountains but especially government, says the Lord. We have seen the exposure of racism and other corruption in Arts and Entertainment with the Sony hacking. We have seen the exposure of unfair treatment and bullying on both sides of the racial divide in the city of Ferguson, MO. Plus other unfortunate deaths of black youths. In 2015, we will see corruption exposed in the church as well.

May the Lord bless you and keep you in 2015!
Dr. Charles Robinson

December 31st, 2014

APPENDIX C: "Melchizedek" and "Salem" Etymologies

מלכי־צדק

The use of a hyphen in a name is quite unusual, and although Melchizedek seems a personal name, it looks more like a title. It consists of two elements, the first one taken from the noun מלך (*melek*), meaning king:

Abarim Publications Theological Dictionary

מלך

The noun מלך (*melek*) is usually translated as king but is in fact "the most common word for chief magistrate," as HAW Theological Wordbook of the Old Testament puts it. Israel's monarchy was predicted long before it was established (See Deuteronomy 17:15), but Israel's king was by no means meant to be an almighty tyrant. What makes the Hebrew royalty unique among the nations is that Israel's monarchy was far removed from the priesthood (See 1 Samuel 13:12-14). This preceded the West's creed of church and state separation by over three millennia.

The word מלך (*melek*) is such an important word in the Bible that it occurs more than 2,500 times and has several distinct derivations, most notably:

- The verb מלך (*malak*), to be or become king.

Other derivations are:

- מלכה (*malka*), meaning queen, which occurs 35 times in Scriptures. HAW notes that the overwhelming majority of these occurrences denote foreigners, sometimes heads of state (1 Kings 10:1) but often ladies associated with a foreign monarchy but without formal authority themselves (Esther 1:9, Daniel 5:10).
- מלכת (*meleket*), also meaning queen, and probably the same as the previous word but in an old fashioned spelling (even for Biblical times). It occurs only one time in the Bible, in Jeremiah 7:18, where it denotes some "queen of heaven". Perhaps Meleketh was her

name or perhaps Jeremiah is facetiously speaking of her in a lofty old tongue.
- **מלוכה** (*meluka*), meaning kingship or royalty.
- **מלכות** (*malkut*), meaning sovereign power.
- **ממלכה** (*mamlaka*), meaning sovereignty, or literally "that in which kingship is manifested."
- **ממלכות**(*mamlakut*), also meaning sovereignty.

However, in Nehemiah 5:7, there occurs an alternate (Aramaic?) usage of the root **מלך** (*malak*), now with the meaning of to consult, or rather intense introspection. Experts state that this particular word comes from an entirely separate root, but these same experts can't really explain how the verbal idea of royalty was formed, or that of intense introspection for that matter.

Note that the Torah includes rules and restrictions specifically for the king, which in itself is highly unusual if not wholly without precedent in the old world. A king had to be chosen by YHWH and not by the people (Deuteronomy 17:15). He couldn't be a foreigner (Deut. 17:15), he couldn't "multiply horses" (in order to lean on military might? Deut. 17:16), he couldn't sport a harem (to prevent distraction, but perhaps also to not unfairly flood the gene pool) or otherwise enrich himself (Deut. 17:17). The one and only thing the king of Israel was supposed to do was to create a copy of the Law with his own hands and meditate on his copy all the days of his life (Deut.17:18-19).

Perhaps these two concepts of to be a king and to consult are not all that far removed, or were not removed in Biblical times, and these similar words are similar because they mean similar things.

The second part of the name Melchizedek comes from the verb **צדק** (*sadeq*), meaning to be just:

Abarim Publications Theological Dictionary

צדק

APPENDIX C

The verb צדק (*sadeq*) means to be just, righteous. According to HAW Theological Wordbook of the Old Testament, "This root basically connotes conformity to an ethical or moral standard."

Such an important verb obviously occurs all over the Bible. It's used in the sense of having a just cause (Job 9:15), being justified (Job 11:2, Isaiah 43:9), or being just in a general sense. (Psalm 51:4, Job 10:15). It's used in a statutory sense (2 Samuel 15:4), a vindictive sense (Deuteronomy 25:1), even a vindicating sense (Isaiah 50:8) and redemptive sense (Daniel 12:3, Genesis 44:16).

Besides this verb, the root yields a few other important derivatives:

- The adjective צדיק (*saddiq*) means just or righteous (Genesis 7:1, 2 Samuel 23:3).
- The masculine noun צדק (*sedeq*), meaning justice or rightness (Deuteronomy 25:15, Leviticus 19:15).
- The feminine noun צדקה (*sadaqa*), meaning righteousness (Isaiah 5:7, Psalm 36:6).

The Name Salem in the Bible

Abarim Publications Theological Dictionary

Salem is the place where Melchizedek was housed (Genesis 14:18). After the war of Four against Five Kings, Abraham's nephew Lot is abducted, and Abraham sets out with a small army to rescue him. As they rescue Lot, they loot the abductors while they're at it and bring back the spoils. This evokes gratitude with the locals among whom is King Melchizedek of Salem.

Melchizedek achieves legendary status in the Bible also because the town called Salem is renamed at some point and becomes known as Jerusalem. According to Psalm 76:2, God's tabernacle is in Salem. The name Salem appears twice but in only one passage in the Greek New Testament and this in conjunction with Melchizedek (spelled Σαλημ; Hebrews 7:1-2).

Etymology of the Name Salem

Originally the name Salem probably had to do with a Ugaritic god, but transliterated this name neatly concurs with the Hebrew verb שלם (*shalem*) meaning to be complete, sound, and the familiar noun שלום(*shalom*), meaning peace:

Abarim Publications Theological Dictionary

שלם

The general meaning of the graceful root-verb שלם(*shalem*) is that of wholeness, completeness or "unbrokenness" (and see for the opposite the verb רעע, *ra'a*). Our verb is used to characterize the uncut stones of the altar (Deuteronomy 27:6) and the temple (1 Kings 6:7). It tells of a "full" or perhaps "righteous" wage (Ruth 1:12), and the entirety of a population (Amos 1:6). It also tells of "full" and just weights, which are God's delight (Deuteronomy 25:15 and Proverbs 11:1), and of "whole" hearts devoted to the Lord (1 Kings 8:61). This verb may even denote the completeness of sin (Genesis 15:16) and in some rare cases it may denote friendship (Jeremiah 20:10, Psalm 41:10).

In the Hebrew language, it's quite simple to indicate not only a condition (like *shalem*), but also the means to get there (to "*shalemize*"). The usage of this *shalemize* form in Scriptures is quite revealing. Wholeness is achieved or restored most often by some kind of restitutory payment or covenant: God pays a man according to his work (Job 34:11), but the wicked borrows and does not pay back (Psalm 37:21). The owner of an accidentally killed ox is paid restitution (Exodus 21:36); oil is sold to pay off a debt (2 Kings 4:7); and the Gibeonites swindle Joshua into making a covenant with them (Joshua 10:1). Likewise, *shalem* is used when vows are to be paid to the Most High, or when days of mourning are to be completed (Isaiah 60:20), and ties in directly to the Messiah and His salvific work (Joel 2:25).

The derivatives of this root-verb are:

- The famous masculine noun שלום (*shalom*), meaning peace (Isaiah 32:17, Psalm 49). Peace in the Bible doesn't just indicate a warless state, but rather a state of completeness and harmony or rather undividedness. It also covers completeness (Jeremiah 13:19), prosperity (Genesis 43:27), health and safety (Psalm 38:4).
- The masculine noun שלם (*shelem*) is a peace offering or a sacrifice for alliance or friendship (Amos 5:22, Exodus 24:5).

APPENDIX C

- The denominative verb שלם (*shalam*), means to be in a covenant of peace (Job 22:21, Isaiah 42:19).
- The adjective שלם (*shalem*), the meaning is perfect, whole, complete, safe (Genesis 15:16, Genesis 33:18, Genesis 34:21).
- The masculine noun שלם (*shillem*), the meaning is recompense (occurs only in Deuteronomy 32:35).
- The masculine noun שלמן (*shalmon*), meaning bribe or reward. This noun only occurs in plural and only in Isaiah 1:23.
- The masculine noun שלום (*shillum*) also spelled שלם (*shillum*), meaning recompense or reward (Isaiah 34:8, Micah 7:3).
- The feminine noun שלמה (*shilluma*), meaning reward (Psalm 91:8 only).

Peace and How to Make it

Some of the nouns derived from this root verb may be construed to mean literally "peacemaker," but that requires some additional considerations. Peace—defined as the absence of conflict or discord—may be achieved in several ways:

- By suppressing certain elements of society, particularly those elements that cause trouble to the ruling elite. That's not what this root means.

- By suppressing certain elements in people's personal mentalities, convictions or behaviors. That's also not what this root means.

- By achieving such a level of understanding of irreconcilable elements that these can be understood and joined in, as well as given the opportunity to derive their identity from, a unified theory or system of definition. This process requires no censoring and demonstrates all elements to be most intimately related to the identity of the whole. The key word of this process is relationship. That's what this root means.

In Hebrew, peacemaking means whole-making, and not warm-fuzzy-deny-your-concerns-and-stop-being-difficult-making. Hebrew peace-making requires the effortful acquisition of intimate knowledge of one's opponent, and since in Hebrew love-making is pretty much the same as knowing someone (the verb ידע, *yada'*, means both to know and to have sex; it's this verb that's used in Genesis 4:1 to explain how Adam and Eve came up with Cain), the command to "love your enemy" (Matthew 5:44) has not a lick to do with placidly suffering abuse and trying to conjure up lofty feelings for the brute who's mistreating you and everything to do with studying your enemy until you know enough about him to either appreciate his motives (and behave in such a compatible way that he stops assaulting you) or else blow him out of the water by being superior.

When Jesus says, "Blessed are the peacemakers" (Matthew 5:9), He does not refer to those people who insist we should all assume a state of blissful indifference, but rather to those people who grab the bull by the horns and stare deep into another's eyes and pick his brain with an axe. Making peace starts with making a relationship with your enemy, and it results in getting to know your enemy (which in turn makes for an excellent chance that at some point your enemy will stop being your enemy).

Mugs and Donuts

Biblical peacemaking is very rare in our world. Critics have noted with some dismay that hallowed tools like social media make the rampant polarization of humanity only worse. And most modern religions, well, are so obsessed with their own image that they suck eggs at making peace. But in the ever-helpful field of mathematics exists a discipline called topology, which studies the kinship of spacial forms. It appears that you can make a donut into a coffee mug by just stretching and twisting it a bit but without doing any ripping or gluing. (Because both the donut and the mug have only one hole, the center hole of the donut becomes the hole of the ear of the mug.)

And that means that if you want to know if two forms are related and might, by some process, be turned into each other *without essentially changing*, all you have to do is count the holes (or in nerd-speak: to determine the geometric genus). Biblical peacemaking does exactly that: it counts the holes (it determines the theometric genus) and shows if and how one theory, or *modus operandi*, can be turned into another, previously held incompatible version. (Like say, turning the mug of Islam into the donut of Christianity).

Evolutionists utilize a similar kinship-finding technique and call it homology—the discipline that demonstrates the structural correlation between body parts, such as a human hand (mug) and a whale's flipper (donut).

More is Less and Less is More

Physicists too are insatiable *shalemists*. Electricity and magnetism were once held to be two completely unrelated forces until Maxwell came along and showed that they are just two sides of the same coin. Since Maxwell's work, electricity (mug) and magnetism (donut) live happily ever after in a theory that describes the unified force of electromagnetism. A while later, people figured out another elementary force by which the universe works, and this became known as the Weak Nuclear Force. Some intricate peacemaking ensued, and the Weak Nuclear Force was shown to be one side of a coin of which Electromagnetism was the other side, this namely the unified Electroweak Force.

The Electroweak Force was examined in relation to a third fundamental force, named the Strong Nuclear Force, and sure enough, they could be combined into the Strong-Electroweak Force. The fourth fundamental force of the universe is Gravity, and although many of science's best and brightest have tried to marry Gravity and the Strong Electroweak Force into the Grand Unified Theory (properly abbreviated as GUT), which is really science's monotheistic deity. (See our peacemaking article on Islam that duly peeves all the right people.) For a fun-filled introduction to the four forces of nature, read our article on the Standard Model of Elementary Particles.

But all these complications aside, a sure sign that a wisdom seeker is on the right track is that his theory is getting smaller and smaller while describing more and more. And conversely, if one's total theory library gets bigger and bigger whilst covering less and less (due to the emergence of commentaries that cast doubt on previous theories), one has surely missed an essential point and might as well take up roulette. Knowledge describes the notes; wisdom describes the symphony.

The verb שלם (*shalem*) denotes a unification that preserves the identity and qualities of the unified elements.

APPENDIX D: History of Jerusalem

Source: http://www.generationword.com/jerusalem101/16-salem-jebus.html

When Abraham entered the land of Canaan around 2000 BC, the city of Jerusalem was called Salem (See Genesis 14). After Abram returned from defeating Kedorlaomer and the kings allied with him, the king of Sodom came out to meet him in the Valley of Shaveh (that is, the King's Valley). Then Melchizedek king of Salem brought out bread and wine. He was the priest of God Most High, and he blessed Abram, saying, "Blessed be Abram by God Most High, Creator of heaven and earth. And blessed be God Most High, who delivered your enemies into your hand." Then Abram gave him a tenth of everything. (Genesis 14:17-20).

Melchizedek's city was called Salem, or Shalem, which is also the name of the God whose worship was centered in the city. The full name of this God was God Most High (El Elyon)—Creator of heaven and Earth since He was the God of creation. It is interesting to note that Abram recognizes this God in verse 22 when he swears by his name and, at the same time, calls Him "Lord" which is the word YHWH, the name of the covenant God of Israel. Abram said to the king of Sodom, "I have raised my hand to the Lord (YHWH), God Most High, Creator of heaven and earth, and have taken an oath that I will accept nothing belonging to you." (Genesis 14:22-23)

Salem, Jebus, Jerusalem, the City of

The original name of the city Jerusalem was "Yerushalem." We already know that "shalem" comes from the name of the God worshiped in the city by Melchizedek. (The Jews taught that Melchizedek was Noah's son Shem, who, according to Biblical records, was still alive at this time.) The word "yeru" means "foundation stone" or "cornerstone." The name Jerusalem, then, means "the foundation stone of Shalem" and refers to the

APPENDIX D

original cornerstone laid by the Creator of the Universe when He built the earth.

Melchizedek was the king of this city, which was located on the southern part of the Eastern Hill between the Kidron Valley and the Central Valley. Abraham met Melchizedek in the Valley of Shaveh that is the King's Valley (Genesis 14:17). This meeting would have been at the south end of the ridge of the city where the Kidron and Hinnom valleys meet. Melchizedek was also a priest of God Most High, who was Abraham's God as well.

Abraham was in Jerusalem again a few years later when he offered Isaac on Mount Moriah, as described in Genesis 22. Mount Moriah is on the northern end of the Eastern Hill that Melchizedek's city sat upon. So, in Genesis 14, Abraham met Melchizedek on the south end of the Eastern Hill in the valley, but in Genesis 22 he went to the highest point, the north end, of that same ridge.

Around the time of Jacob and Joseph (1800-1700 BC), Jerusalem, or Rushalimum, is mentioned in an Egyptian text as a chief city in the central hill country with two rulers named Y'qar'am and Shas'an. Just a few years later in another Egyptian text, the name Jerusalem is mentioned along with the name of one single ruler, which is illegible.

Canaanites continued to live in the city through the days of Abraham, Isaac, Jacob, and Jacob's twelve sons. After the Hebrews spent 400 years in Egypt and 40 years in the wilderness, Joshua led them into the Promised Land. The Jebusites (also called Amorites) were a group of Canaanites. The king's name at that time was Adonizedek (Joshua 10:1-3) who appears to be an heir or descendent of Melchizedek. (Notice the common spelling: Melchi-zedek.) The Zedek family, or the Zedek title, had been in those ruling Jerusalem from 2000 to 1400 BC. In about the year 1404 BC, Adonizedek met Joshua on that fateful day when the sun stood still and was killed by Joshua (Joshua 10:3; 12:7, 10). Joshua continued to lead the Israelites through the wilderness into this Promised Land given to Abraham by God.

After Joshua's death, the men of Judah attacked and captured Jerusalem. The people in the city were slaughtered, and the city was burnt. The men of Judah attacked Jerusalem also and took it. They put the city to the sword and set it on fire. (Judges 1:8). After that time, the city of Jerusalem was resettled by Jebusites. The city was named Jebus by its inhabitants. Judah could not dislodge the Jebusites, who were living in Jerusalem; to this day the Jebusites live there with the people of Judah. (Joshua 15:63). The Amarna Collection was found in Egypt in 1887. It is a collection of ancient letters written on clay tablets varying in size from 2 x 2.5 inches up to 3.5 x 9 inches.

A substantial amount of the content of these letters written to Pharaoh Amenhotep III (1410-1377 BC) are appeals from many of the kings in Canaan for military help and provisions. At that time, the land of Canaan was being overrun by invaders referred

APPENDIX D

to in the letters as "Haibru." The word "Habiru" simply means "nomadic invaders," but its pronunciation sounds like the name of a people called "Hebrews" known to have invaded the same land of Canaan in a similar fashion at the very same time. The Exodus of the Hebrews from Egypt is dated as occurring in the year 1444 BC. After forty years in the wilderness, the Hebrews would have entered Canaan in 1405-1404 BC. For the next seventy years, letters written from the land of Canaan focus on the chaos and fighting caused by these Habiru invaders.

The original tablet is preserved in the Vorderasiatisches Museum in Berlin. Recently in June 2010, Eilat Mazar found a clay fragment from this same period in the area of the Ophel in Jerusalem written in the same style cuneiform on Jerusalem clay by a royal scribe. This find confirms Egypt's opinion of Jerusalem, as portrayed in the Amarna Letters, as a major city even centuries before David's conquest of it. The Royal Archives

APPENDIX D

of Tel Al-Amarna, Egypt, contained 350 letters written in cuneiform script. This clay tablet is one of six letters written to Egyptian kings by the ruler of Jerusalem shortly after 1400 BC. Jerusalem is called "Urusalim" in these Amarna Letters. Joshua had recently killed a king of Jerusalem (Joshua 12:7-10). The city name "Urusalim" means "foundation of Shalem." The deity's name, "Shalem," means "complete," "prosperous," and "peaceful" as seen in the text of Hebrews 7:2 where "king of Salem" means "king of peace."

A letter sent to Pharaoh Amenhotep IV of Egypt between 1350 and 1334 BC from Jerusalem has survived among the Amarna letters. The letter is from Abdi-Hepa, the ruler of Jerusalem, which indicates that Jerusalem was an important city at that time. In these letters, Abdi-Hepa, a Hittite name, discusses a failed attempt to break into his palace to assassinate him. The natural location of this palace fortress would be the same place in Jerusalem that the kings before him and after him would choose: the north edge of the city near the Ophel. (David would eventually take this fortress around 1005 BC). In these letters also the ruler of Jerusalem is clearly having trouble with invaders and raiding parties a generation after Joshua brought Israel into the land of Canaan. Abdi-Hepa was asking for help from the Egyptian Pharaoh.

Jebus, or Jerusalem, is also mentioned in the account of a traveling Levite in the book of Judges from roughly around 1200 BC. Unwilling to stay another night, the man left and went toward Jebus (that is, Jerusalem), with his two saddled donkeys and his concubine. When they neared Jebus and the day was almost gone, the servant said to his master, "Come, let's stop at this city of the Jebusites and spend the night." His master replied, "No. We won't go into an alien city whose people are not Israelites. We will go on to Gibeah." (Judges 19:10-12).

By David's day in 1005 BC, these Jebusites had built up the southern half of the Eastern Hill. The Jebusites had built walls around their city and had added considerable defensive structures on the north end in the middle of the Eastern Hill in the area called the Ophel. The northern section of the ridge, Mount Moriah, was being used as a threshing floor (2 Samuel 24:16-24). This city covered about ten acres.

When David was 37-years-old and had reigned in Hebron for seven years, his men entered the city of Jerusalem through the water system and took it from the Jebusites. (2 Samuel 5:4-9). David began extensive building in Jerusalem which he renamed "the City of David." The Bible says that David captured the "stronghold of Jerusalem," which would be the same palace fortress mentioned by Adbi-Hepa and used for centuries by the kings who proceeded David:

The Jebusites said to David, "You will not get in here. . . ." Nonetheless, David did capture the fortress of Zion, the City of David. David then took up residence in the fortress and called it the City of David. He built up the area around it, from the supporting terraces (Millo) inward. (2 Samuel 5:6-7, 9.)

Spirit-Led Publishing

↑Spirit-Led
⇞Publishing

Go to spiritledpublishing.com

Select "**Tell me how inexpensively and professionally you can publish my book.**"

In this season of the end-time, it is absolutely critical that the *arrows of intercession that we shoot hit the mark all the time.*

The prophet Jeremiah spoke these words: "**Yes, prepare to attack Babylon, all you nations round about. Let your *archers* shoot at her. *Spare no arrows*, for she has sinned against the Lord.**" (Jeremiah 50:14.)

Spirit-Led Publishing is your full service publishing house. We help publish your Spirit-Led "Master Pieces."

Let your "arrows"—your books—hit their mark. Launch them through Spirit-Led Publishing.

Notes

More from WISE Ministries:

WISE Prayer Request Website and Theme Song

www.coachmybusiness.com/prayer-request.php

WISE Online Store Links for DVDs

DVDs from WISE provided to Certification Course Students:
Intercession 2.0.
Taking Company to Next Level Spiritually
Opening Global Gates of Access

Tipping Point Media

Tipping Point 2013 Gathering Conference DVD (also available on CD and MP3)

For information and to register for monthly gatherings:

http://www.tippingpointnw.com/

Site to purchase Let Heaven Invade the Seven Mountains of Culture:
http://www.LetHeavenInvade7M.com/

Site to purchase Melchizedek books and everything Melchizedek:
Melchizedek.International

About the Author

Dr. Charles Robinson and his wife, Liz Robinson, have pioneered global breakthrough in the field of marketplace ministry through WISE Ministries International. WISE empowers leaders by providing a combination of business, spiritual, and prophetic support. The Robinsons employ their impressive history of schooling and degrees with their multifaceted experience in ministry and in business as foundations from which to guide others. Both Charles and Liz are ordained ministers with CIAN, Christian International Apostolic Network, and they serve as current directors of IAMIN, Seven Mountains University, and Melchizedek International. The Robinsons maintain offices in Hollywood, CA; Washington DC; and Shenzhen, China to personally minister on the mountains of business, entertainment, and government. Charles also is the man who convenes the biannual Tipping Point Gathering 7-UP Unconference—this an interactive three-day meeting of key leaders from all seven mountains of cultural influence.

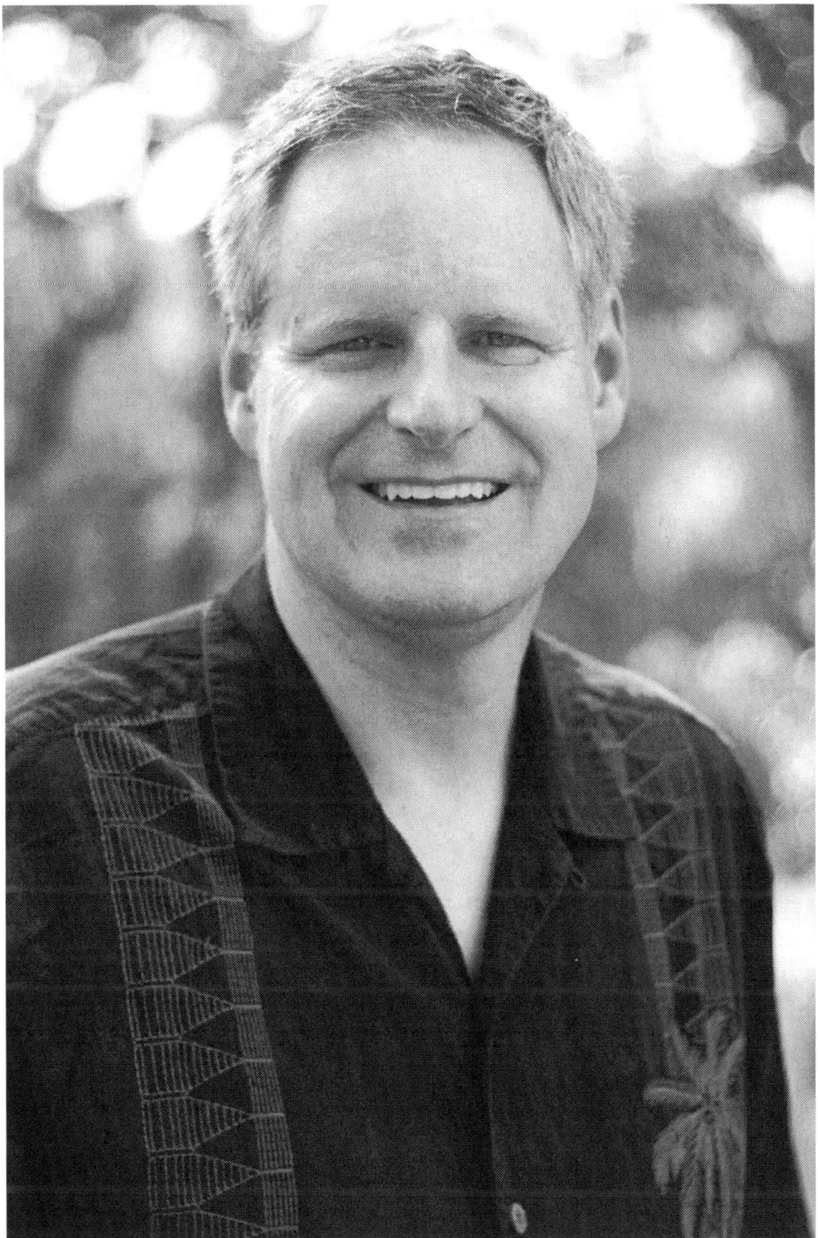

Made in the USA
San Bernardino, CA
29 December 2015